Each Day

Each Day

A Veteran Educator's
Guide to Raising Children

Z. Vance Wilson

ROWMAN & LITTLEFIELD
Lanham · Boulder · New York · London

All permissions and copyright information appear at the end of the book.

Published by Rowman & Littlefield
A wholly owned subsidiary of The Rowman & Littlefield Publishing Group, Inc.
4501 Forbes Boulevard, Suite 200, Lanham, Maryland 20706
www.rowman.com

Unit A, Whitacre Mews, 26-34 Stannary Street, London SE11 4AB

Distributed by NATIONAL BOOK NETWORK

British Library Cataloguing in Publication Information Available

Library of Congress Cataloging-in-Publication Data Available

978-1-4758-2776-7 (cloth)
978-1-4758-2777-4 (electronic)

∞™ The paper used in this publication meets the minimum requirements of American National Standard for Information Sciences—Permanence of Paper for Printed Library Materials, ANSI/NISO Z39.48-1992.

Printed in the United States of America

To my children, Evan and Emily Wilson
And in memory of my father, mother, and brother

Contents

Foreword

David Ignatius

$\mathcal{I}$n medieval times, scholars sometimes spoke of a "great chain of being," which described the faith and traditions that had been passed from generation to generation. Boys' preparatory schools—modern survivors of medieval times—have something similar in the body of knowledge that's passed from headmaster to headmaster. This accumulated wisdom may seem to outsiders as arcane as a spell from Hogwarts, but it's an encyclopedia of life.

The headmaster in the years I was a student at St. Albans, Canon Charles Martin, wrote missives home to parents (and boys, but we got the message orally several times a day). They were eventually gathered into a book, *Letters from a Headmaster's Study*. His basic admonition to boys and parents alike was that they should seek admission to the Kingdom of Heaven, not the kingdom of Harvard. Woe unto those who got the applications mixed up. Canon Martin rarely referred to Jesus by name; instead, he spoke simply of "the Teacher."

I think of this collection of essays by Vance Wilson, the current headmaster of St. Albans, as a successor to Canon Martin's book. It is a link in our great chain of being. It's about the permanent things—the values we try to teach our children or, if we're lucky, that we encounter in an educator like Charles Martin or Vance Wilson.

The *New Yorker* writer John McPhee wrote a book, called *The Headmaster*, about Frank Boyden, who was head of Deerfield Academy for sixty-six years. Boyden, he said, was part of "a skein of magnanimous despots . . . who created enduring schools through their own individual energies." Vance Wilson is part of that skein, too. He's too modern a man to seem autocratic, and headmasters these days can get sued if they let their inner despot become too obvious. But Boyden would recognize Wilson as a member of his own

ancient fraternity of educators who teach boys to become men by emphasiz-
ing—insisting upon—values that endure.

Boyden explained to McPhee how he ran his school: "My philosophy—I
can't express it, really: I believe in boys. I believe in keeping them busy, and in
the highest standards of scholarship. I believe in a very normal life. It generally seeps in. I try to do the simple things that a well-organized home does
for its boys."

A similar humility and belief shapes these essays. As headmaster, Wilson thinks carefully about what boys must understand about life if they are
to become whole, morally and intellectually. He leans against the ephemeral
values that surround his students and tries to communicate what is real and
enduring. He's their last chance, in a sense, before they're buried by college
and adult life.

In these letters, speeches, and homilies, Wilson shares the things he has
learned from books, prayer, and his own boyhood in the mountains of North
Carolina. He writes from the heart, always: about how prisoners manage to
survive unspeakable captivity; about the motivations of the anonymous hero
who reaches out to save others in a freezing river, giving up his own life; about
"listening to the stars" in what feels like an empty universe.

Wilson writes about the particular things that are essential knowledge
at a boys' school: what real toughness is; what makes boys different from
girls; why boys need to choose their band of brothers wisely. He describes
the enduring, unfair, but inescapable attraction of the wayward prodigal son,
compared to his virtuous, dutiful older brother; he explains the need in our
lives for laughter, even the teasing, occasionally cruel kind that is an eternal
feature of prep-school life; he asserts the value of silence (turn off your cell
phones!). One of the most important essays in this book explains why high-
achieving parents must avoid poisoning their children with too much love and
ambition. (He aptly cites the old saw: "The easiest way to kill a houseplant
is to overwater it.")

Wilson turns often to the Bible for his stories. He's not an ordained
minister, unlike most of his St. Albans headmaster predecessors, but he
sometimes thinks like one. He writes often about prayer; he cites stories about
Jesus and other passages from scripture. He is rooted in his faith tradition,
but not insistent on it. As someone once said of the Episcopal Church, his
faith is solid at the core but loose at the edges. I think that's part of why St.
Albans works: It can reach for universal values because it stands firmly in its
own traditions.

Wilson loves good writing, as the reader will see from his own evoca-
tive prose and the writers he cites. Some are from his beloved South, such
as Thomas Wolfe and Flannery O'Connor; others are modern writers, like

poets Richard Wilbur or W.H. Auden, or the playwright Arthur Miller; some are immortals like Homer and Dostoyevsky. Wilson's most moving piece of exegesis may be his reading of Maurice Sendak's *Where the Wild Things Are*. This rich, diverse literary culture is part of the great chain of being that Wilson embodies.

My favorite passages in this book are the stories from Wilson's childhood in Asheville, North Carolina. He remembers the texture of his boyhood: reading the Bible, failing exams, learning at the feet of his father and his "hero" grandfather, who was a country railroad conductor evidently beloved by every passenger. The most moving stories are about Wilson's favorite "Uncle Turk," a charismatic combat veteran of World War II who suffered from alcoholism.

Wilson never brags about himself. You wouldn't know from these essays that he was a star basketball player at Yale. The implicit lesson is that real men don't brag.

Wilson celebrates many sons of his school, great achievers like the actor Jeffrey Wright or the Hall of Fame pro football star Jonathon Ogden. But he gives special place to a St. Albans graduate who died in service to his country: James Harvey Gaul, who parachuted behind German lines as an O.S.S. intelligence officer in World War II and was captured and killed.

In these essays, you will enter a St. Albans School that is a very particular place. It is unapologetically an Episcopal Church school, in the shadow of the inspiring, humbling Washington National Cathedral. It's a place where students get used to the peal of bells from the great tower of the cathedral, and ingest at chapel services the hymns of the fat Episcopal Hymnal and the thinner Book of Common Prayer. Habit can become faith: When my first grandchild was born, and I was trying to sing her to sleep, I found myself singing the hymns I had sung every morning as a boy. My little granddaughter's earliest memories may be the words, "Turn Back, O Man!"

I attended St. Albans from 1962 to 1968. The school shaped me, in more powerful and also subtler ways than I realized at the time. I was baptized, confirmed, and married on the cathedral close. My three children were baptized there. I have attended many memorial services there for beloved friends, and I hope someday that my friends will gather there to say goodbye to me. The school and its traditions are imprinted on me, along with the words of the school hymn, gruff admonitions from my football coach Glenn Wild, and especially, words from my headmaster.

The voice of the headmaster never really leaves us. What this boy remembers best from his senior year isn't getting into college, or even his first girlfriend, but making a tackle in the final minutes of the Landon game, a lucky "form tackle" in front of the St. Albans bench, and having the headmaster greet him the rest of senior year with a vice-like grip on the neck and the words, "Hey, there, tackler."

Wilson writes in the knowledge that his voice will echo in memory for his boys. As his title conveys, it's a message conveyed by headmaster, and heard by the boys, "each day."

Perhaps people will decide someday that boys' prep school are too archaic a relic of the past and turn St. Albans into something else. I hope not. But they should understand that, whatever its elite status, the school is about service, and what it was once common to call "manly virtue."

Most graduates could probably sing with me, from memory, the first stanza of the school hymn: "Men of the future stand, and watch each fleeting hour, to make your lives what God has planned and spread abroad His power." That's the tradition that was entrusted to Wilson when he became headmaster. As readers will see, he has added new links to the chain that are intensely personal, honest self-reckonings. They express the moral character that the headmaster of a great school seeks to share with his wider family.

Preface

$\mathcal{I}$ became headmaster of St. Albans School in Washington, D.C., in 1999. Founded in 1909, the all-boys' school is part of the Protestant Episcopal Cathedral Foundation, which includes the Washington National Cathedral; the Cathedral Elementary School, Beauvoir; and, the National Cathedral School (NCS) for Girls, with which St. Albans has a coordinate relationship. This work would not be possible without the steadfast support of the St. Albans Governing Boards, the trustees of the foundation, my fellow school heads at NCS and Beauvoir, and the pastoral care of four bishops of the diocese of Washington and four deans of the cathedral. Yes, St. Albans is part of a complicated place, and I leave it at that. Most of all, led by my colleagues on the St. Albans faculty, the community of parents and students and alumni have shown great patience with my efforts and encouraged me in my work.

I write letters in many formats to our constituents, preach in the Little Sanctuary (our chapel) and on occasion in the cathedral, and give speeches, primarily to parents but also to others. While this is a collection culled from these writing and speaking events over the years, I have tried to link ideas and edit out repetitions before the indulgent reader suffers early onset of nausea. I thank in particular the generation of boys who listened to me, most of whom stayed awake.

I
ENCOURAGING HEROISM

· 1 ·

A Humane Intelligence

A good head and a good heart are always a formidable combination.

—Nelson Mandela

*W*hen winter came, the temperature fell to thirty-five degrees below zero. The Soviet prison camp's handbook described the wind as a "satanic blast of untamable force that . . . gathered speed in the limitless expanses of the steppe where it met no obstacles." For a bricklayer, the mortar froze. If his bare hand stuck fast to the bricks, his skin tore off when he pulled his hand away. He had to darn his own mittens. He also had to sew his identification number on each piece of clothing and, if necessary, scrounge around for scrap material to patch the holes that cut out the numbers. For the rest of Alexander Solzhenitsyn's life, those numbers symbolized the humiliation and dehumanization of the prison camp, for a guard never called him by name, only by number.

Besides being tough, Solzhenitsyn was lucky, as he was the first to admit. Disease did not kill him, a camp guard did not beat him to death, and a fellow prisoner did not cut his throat. He was able to learn how to survive the cold, the daily gruel, and the standard abuse, and to learn his given task: to build brick walls, which over time he did with energy and pride. But each survivor of a prison camp testifies that, to live, he had to do more than his allotted task, or he would go crazy from boredom and disillusionment: There were those who stole, those who bullied fellow prisoners, and those who plotted to murder stool pigeons. There were those who survived off memories from home, and those who deeply cared for fellow prisoners in danger.

Always known as an odd man, Solzhenitsyn, to survive, began collecting broken matches. During the day he laid out two rows of ten pieces of matchstick on his cigarette case below the brick wall he was building, and at night on his bed. The lower row represented a unit of ten and the higher a unit of one, abacus-like. Then he silently began reciting poetry he had learned in school, and later he recited poetry that he had written earlier in his life, moving from the bottom row one stick for every one line he remembered and from the top row another stick once he recited ten lines. Somehow this worked. After a while, he found scraps of paper and pencil stubs, and at night he composed new lines, and the next day he stuck some of those scraps into the mortar along the brick wall until he had memorized the new lines and could destroy the evidence. Then some Catholic Lithuanians who befriended him made him a rosary, with one hundred beads not forty, and each tenth bead cubical and the hundredth bead heart-shaped. Now as he recited, the guards assumed he was praying. By the time he was released from the camp, he had memorized twelve thousand lines of poetry, a feat reminiscent of medieval and ancient poets who worked in the oral tradition. For example, and to put this in perspective, there are 12,110 lines in *The Odyssey*.

And so he lived. His autobiographical poem began to document life in the labor camps and memorialized those who died unknown and in unmarked mass graves. His work on the poem would in time lead to a seminal political work of the last century, *The Gulag Archipelago*. It shocked the world, for in the West it was only rumored that these people lived and died, at least in the kind of numbers Solzhenitsyn asserted. The numbers were first disbelieved. He argued that sixty million people died in Stalin's camps. Add together the deaths in World War I and World War II—that's approximately sixty million.

Nelson Mandela was born the same year as Solzhenitsyn, 1918. Prison routines around the world mimic each other. Of the twenty-seven years he was incarcerated, Mandela spent nineteen in the Robben Island prison, off the coast of Cape Town, South Africa. He, too, always wore a number, but also the letter *D*, as in *dog*, the lowest of the prison's four ranks, because he was a political prisoner. No one was thought more dangerous than a political prisoner. Thus, he was given the smallest rations, smaller than those given to fellow political prisoners who were white.

Mandela was courageous; he also believed he was fortunate. Like his inspiration, Mahatma Gandhi, he struggled, not against a political party with murderous oligarchs, but against an oppressor who had a legal system, even if prejudicial, even if supported by murderous secret military services. South African society was more open to the world than the Soviet towns and camps in Siberia. Nevertheless, he still had to survive the tin-cup rations, the hammering labor, the ceaseless boredom, and the vile prejudice. Though a well-educated man and the great-grandson of a king, he too had to learn a new job—to go to a lime quarry every day and break apart rocks. Like Solzhenitsyn, he kept up the pace and did his job.

More people survived Robben Island than the Soviet camps, but each survivor testifies that, to survive, he had to do more than eat and drink and break apart rocks: Some started a black market or betrayed their fellow prisoners, others lived each day only for the possibility of a soccer game at day's end or perhaps for an occasional letter made nearly unreadable by the censors, and some cared for each other or debated the merits of the South African Communist Party or the African National Committee.

Nelson Mandela went back to school, from his jail cell. He wanted to add new letters to his numbers and the letter *D*; he wanted a J.D. (doctor of jurisprudence) to follow his B.A. (bachelor of arts), so through a correspondence course with the University of London, he obtained a law degree. But that was not all. During his studies and afterward, he always taught his fellow prisoners, this act of teaching for him an act of survival by educating his compatriots. He was so successful as a teacher that the ruling white government dubbed Robben Island "Mandela University" and eventually removed him for fear of what his teaching might inspire in the prisoners.

One of the best-selling books at the U.S. Holocaust Memorial Museum is *Man's Search for Meaning*, written by the camp survivor and Viennese psychotherapist Viktor Frankl. From 1942 to 1945, Frankl was imprisoned, with numbers sewn into his clothes, in three concentration camps. After the Americans freed Dachau, Frankl devoted the rest of his life to studying the characteristics of those who lived in the camps and those who survived. He argued that the prisoners, when they could gather together, desperately needed a sense that they were not alone, that either there was a loved one mysteriously in their presence and in their memories, or beside them a fellow prisoner they respected and needed, or a divine being looking down on them. We must have food and water and some luck to live, Frankl admitted, but this abiding emotion, this faith that there is meaning in life because it is lived with others, cannot disappear. If so, isolation and disillusionment kill.

Each of these three stories celebrates intellectual accomplishment. Might I suggest, however, that many of the opponents of Solzhenitsyn, Mandela, and Frankl were also brilliant people? The logistics of the Soviet prison camps required organized if evil minds. The Nazi SS leaders gathered at Wansee Lake to create what they imagined was a brilliant Final Solution to gas millions of people. The laws of South Africa's apartheid system so absurdly parsed differences in race that today they read like a stand-up comic routine, but they were the work of the government's best minds.

The intellect, however free to be creative and experimental, must be governed by a sense of humanity and by a profound devotion to community. It must also be supported by a sense of worth and purpose. Solzhenitsyn memorialized the murdered, Mandela educated his compatriots and freed his people, and Frankl helped us find therapeutic meaning in life. Our blood is common, whatever the color of our skin or our cultural background or our political and religious beliefs. Our intellects must establish and sustain human justice against anyone's unjust and brilliant solutions to problems that are imagined out of paranoia and fear. Dear friends, what value does intellectual gain have if not grounded in justice and love?

· 2 ·

Anonymous Heroism

It's something I never thought I'd do, . . . but somebody had to go into the water.

—Lenny Skutnik

On Wednesday, January 13, 1982, an afternoon snowstorm struck Washington, D.C. January had already become a month too long, with days bitter enough to make the ground block hard and to ice the surface of the Potomac River. That Wednesday the snow struck harsh against the face, the sky hung low and depressed us, and people wanted to get home.

Downtown, the afternoon traffic stalled on the bridges across the Potomac. Visibility was only a half mile. Suddenly, from the direction of Washington National Airport, a Boeing 737—Air Florida flight 90—descended toward the 14th Street Bridge. It sheered the tops off some cars, knocked four trucks and cars off the bridge to their drivers' deaths, had a 180-foot section of its fuselage torn off, and tumbled nose down in the middle of the iced-over river. Luggage littered the ice, and the fuselage slowly submerged to its grave. But the tail section, with six people climbing out to its wings, still teetered atop the ice near the bridge.

A National Park Service helicopter got airborne first and attempted a rescue. Its pilot, a man named Donald Usher, maneuvered the rescue helicopter so dangerously close to the river its skids could have iced up and destabilized the craft. His paramedic, Gene Windsor, tossed the copter's single lifeline to the six visible survivors on the severed tail section. The machine had to drag each, one by one, to the shore. But on the way in, one young woman lost her grip and was about to drown, or suffer cardiac arrest—her body temperature was eighty-one degrees Fahrenheit. A man named Lenny Skutnik, watching from the riverside, dove into the freezing river and pulled

7

her close enough to shore for a fireman to swim out and retrieve her. Later Skutnik said, "It's something I never thought I'd do, . . . but somebody had to go into the water."

A fourth hero was not identified for days afterwards. A passenger on the plane, he became known as the anonymous hero, or simply, "the man in the water." He was bald, in his fifties, with what one observer described as "an extravagant moustache." Each time the paramedic, Windsor, tossed the lifeline, this man caught it and the flotation ring. Then he passed it on to someone else. Windsor said, "In a mass casualty, you'll find people like him, but I've never seen one man with that much commitment." After the helicopter had taken every other person on that tail section to safety, it turned back. They wanted to rescue this heroic man who had put others' lives before his own. But by then the cold had killed him, and he had dropped under the icy water to his own death.

Roger Rosenblatt in *Time* magazine wrote, "For at some moment in the water [this man] must have realized that he would not live if he continued to hand over the rope and ring to others. He *had* to know, no matter how gradual the effect of the cold. In his judgment he had no choice. When the helicopter took off with what was to be the last survivor, he watched everything in the world move away from him, and he deliberately let it happen."

On Saturday evening, August 11, 2001—just three weeks before I began writing this—a twenty-four-year-old cabinetmaker named Numa Blanco and his pregnant wife Judy Diaz left their home in their new car to drive down Broad Branch Road toward a restaurant in the District. The torrential rain hadn't stopped all day. Like most people in the city, however, they assumed Washington, D.C., could handle it. Who could imagine this imperial city becoming a disaster zone simply because of rain? Mr. Blanco and Ms. Diaz had not listened to the radio or seen on television the news of storm warnings throughout the District and surrounding counties. On Broad Branch, without warning, they drove into a literal wall of water. Ms. Diaz was driving. She jammed the car in reverse, but it shut off. Her husband jumped out to try to push the car backwards, but when he opened the door, the water poured in. He helped his pregnant wife out of the car, but the water swept her out of his hand. The current then slammed him against the guardrails, out of her sight.

Then Ms. Diaz felt human hands. She felt herself being picked up out of the water and carried back up the hill to a Volvo station wagon. The anonymous man returned to her husband, found him in the swirling water, and pulled him from the water. He backed his station wagon up the hill, turned it around, and drove them to the nearest point of safety, a recreation center where he could telephone Sibley Memorial Hospital for an ambulance. Both were treated for sprains and bruises, but most important, the unborn child was safe. The next day they discovered that their new car had been swept completely down into Rock Creek. Diaz said, "I know that if it wasn't for [that man] . . . we [too] would have been swept away. We would have drowned." The man, however, never identified himself. The only hint they had about who he was shimmered on the back windshield of his car—a St. Albans sticker.

As a writer or a speaker, when you juxtapose two stories the way I have, you have a moral obligation to be clear and fair and not to overreach. (I'm certain the anonymous man in the station wagon would agree.) These stories differ in scale. The first included the deaths of seventy-eight people—the second, no one. The danger in the first was also greater than in the second. The small second story began in the twenty-eighth paragraph of the newspaper's main story about the storms that surprised us, but we all know that small event could have easily turned into a disaster and death. Then it would have been the lead paragraph.

Our sons are growing up in a culture whose five-star, Grammy Award–winning, two-minute drill, Jumbotron message is that the ultimate goal in life is to be a celebrity. We all are subtly taught that the camera is more real than reality. Jesus Christ quickly left the scenes of his miracles. We are to act for the salvation of others, and they act for ours, and in both our doing so, we are saved. Let us remember that man who decades ago let other people survive the crash of Air Florida 90. Let us thank that unknown gentleman from St. Albans who cared enough to risk danger to save the lives of a couple and their unborn child. Let us thank him for quietly stepping away once he realized they would be safe. Every day this year, by the grace of God, in little ways or even in large ways, we can anonymously do the same.

Postscript: Months after the plane crash, the identity of the man in the water was discovered. Only one corpse in the river had lungs full of water: Arland Dean Williams Jr. was the sole person to exit the airplane alive but still die, drowning while saving others. The repaired northbound bridge now bears his name, although most people still refer to it as the 14th Street Bridge. The young alumnus who helped Mr. Blanco and Ms. Diaz came by to see me one afternoon. He preferred to remain anonymous.

• 3 •

Toughness

Let's talk "tough." The culture in which our boys grow up sends a message. Tough is cool.

We often characterize toughness as physical and competitive. Whatever the activity—snowboarding, football, or even quicksilver computer games— the message is more than "be physically strong" but rather "be physically strong enough to waste your opponent." Annihilation, man.

This message implies toughness is emotional strength. You can "waste your opponent" not only if you sharpen your skills but if you stay the course, set aside self-doubt, and, frankly, not think about the result and its damage. Just win or lose. Emotions are tools in the game: *Mine are tougher than yours.*

And winning means you're cool. Advertisers reward you with unnaturally beautiful and brainless women, beer that flows like Colorado cool water, and cars you can drive fast across the mesas of Utah.

But standing alone on a mesa in Utah, at night, transitions us to another kind of toughness. Be patient with me.

In my reading, I've come across an entry from a journal of a high school physics student, a young man of about sixteen who, from what he looked like as an adult, was not a candidate for physical toughness: more a nerd, in my opinion—average face but a lisp and a strange enthusiasm for weird stuff. His entry comes from a journal his science teacher asked him to keep when he was first learning about physics and astronomy.

The question the teacher asked him was, "How would you explain to someone how many stars there are?"

"Sit down and loosen your collar button," he writes (yes, he was indeed a sixteen-year-old nerd but one destined to explain well). "The number in very

round figures is somewhat more than one-hundred-seventy octillion (170,000,
000,000,000,000,000,000,000,000) stars [that's 170 followed by 27 zeroes].

"Take every grain of sand on every beach. Multiply it by ten. That
number is now one-one-hundredth the number of stars in the universe. The
reader now, perhaps, has some idea as to the immensity of the universe."

Thank you, Nerd.

His name was Carl Sagan. Over the course of his life, Sagan wrote
highly regarded publications, received Emmys for his work on television, and
was awarded some of the highest public service medals this country bestows.

But when I imagine one of our boys writing that paragraph at the age
of sixteen, I'm delighted. This young man is trying to solve the problem of
language that every scientist—in fact every thinker—must solve if he wants to
be understood. He's trying to describe the *extra-human*—the size and scope
and mystery of the universe—in human terms. He does so by cleverly dem-
onstrating his numerical literacy—very large round numbers multiplied by
ten which equal a small fraction of the desired quantity—and by making the
abstractions real when he compares the octillion numbers to grains of sand,
which can be touched and is a physical substance ripe with symbolic overtones
which we learn about when we study William Blake the poet or James Joyce
the novelist or Abraham, the father of the Hebrew people. And of course, if
you're standing in the vast openness of a southern Utah mesa staring up at the
night, the stars seems spread across the sky like grains of sand.

Imagine yourself underneath that night sky, in an open space, standing
alone. You look up at those stars and perhaps cup your mouth with your hand
and shout something. Let's say you shout your name.

You wait.

You shout it out again, pitching it toward the stars farthest away in the
sky.

What do you hear back?

Now let's talk "tough."

I imagine some might say, "I hear nothing"; others might say, "I hear
silence"; and still others might say, "I hear the sounds of the night." Another
might say, "What's the point, Headmaster?"

But from the sky you didn't imagine hearing a recognizable human
response, nor did you imagine a divine or supernatural voice calling back affirming who you are or telling you everything is going to be all right.

Did you?

One true measure of a person's real and lasting toughness is how he
responds to what he does not hear back from the stars. All of us can imagine
hearing back. What most of us desire is the voice of an affirming god who

loves us and promises us that after we die we will live in a mysterious, new, and perfect way in a realm we can't explain or know here in our present chronological, three-dimensional lives. That is our hope. For some of us, it is our faith.

But we don't hear that message back in a way our five senses or our rational mind understands. The news from the universe is intimidating. The stars are so infinitesimally small and so far away that by the time their burning light travels the distance to get to where we can see them in the sky, the stars are dead.

You might think me strange, too, but as I said, these facts make me raise the question of just how tough I am. I can strut, I can taunt, I can work out, I can become violent and think my victories cool, I can deny, but what do I do when I do look up—and I believe sooner or later life will force me to look up—and ask who I am? And what will happen to me? Do we actually imagine that we will *never* die?

We drift toward philosophers and theologians. I offer three spiritual alternatives represented by three physical responses. The physical responses (and, of course, there are alternatives) are raise a fist, walk away, or kneel.

Most boys would find the first option—"raise a fist"—attractive. It's so dramatic. It's defiant. It's so dog-poundish-cheering, with the fist up, prancing around with the chest out, taunting the other cheering squad by pointing at them.

If the fist is raised toward the night sky, I interpret the message as something like this: *OK, say that I am nothing compared to this mystery. I am who I am, but I'm proud, and nothing will make me bow. I will raise my fist against everything.*

After he murdered his brother Abel out of jealousy, Cain answered God by saying, "Am I my brother's keeper?" Then he was cursed to wander the earth. And yet many traditions have him wearing the mark of Cain with pride, walking through the earth with his fist raised.

In John Milton's *Paradise Lost,* Satan loses the battle of heaven and is tossed into hell, where he wakes up in the great Furnace. With "obdurate pride" he rallies his fellow devils to continue their revolt against God, concluding his great speech with the ringing lines, "To reign is worth ambition though in Hell / Better to reign in Hell, than serve in Heav'n." That's the best fist-against-the-sky speech ever written. Talk about toughness.

The second physical response to my way of thinking is, I believe, the most common: the act of walking away. When confronted with troubling news in *Gone with the Wind,* Scarlett O'Hara famously answers, "I'll think about that tomorrow." Who was Cleopatra? The Queen of Denial. Most seriously, T. S. Eliot's line "distracted from distraction by distraction" captures something of the obsessive avoidance of our culture, perhaps best seen today by our culture's desire to move us out of nature, where night skies confront us, to sit us in front of screens until we die, and never to allow us any silence.

Our culture certainly doesn't want us to think silence is good or to recognize that silence is free. Silence is not marketed; it's not television or computer or phone or Times Square advertising. It's not jazzy. Just fill yourself up with an octillion mindless things to do, all of which feel good, and walk away from your human condition—until the moment you are dying, and you find yourself asking, "What did life mean? Was I just supposed to keep busy?"

And what if we kneel? What does this third response say? "OK," it seems to say, "instead of raising my fist, I will accept something about our human condition that makes me kneel and pray for something: understanding? grace? the simple human necessity of giving in?" I know this secret: lots of kneeling, of gathering your body toward its center, creates a powerful, physical memory that never disappears.

I argue for an acceptance of the reality that at first and for much of our lives is stark. It can be brutal. I also argue for the truthful acceptance of doubt.

But I believe in kneeling.

And why not one more response, just to make dealing with all this even more challenging? Why not get up to dance and sing? Regardless. What's a better option than that?

Let us become singers or poets of life and, I'm quick to add, pay attention to life. With the Psalmist you say, "Let all the earth keep silent before the Lord." With Gerard Manley Hopkins you say, "The world is charged with the grandeur of God." With W. H. Auden you say, "O who can ever gaze his fill."

I end with an admonition to spend some time reflecting on these last lines of a great Auden poem, "Death's Echo":

> The desires of the heart are as crooked as corkscrews,
>   Not to be born is the best for man;
> The second-best is a formal order,
>   The dance's pattern; Dance while you can.
>
> Dance, dance, for the figure is easy,
>   The tune is catching and will not stop;
> Dance till the stars come down with the rafters;
>   Dance, dance, dance till you drop.

· 4 ·

Band of Brothers

We few, we happy few, we band of brothers; For he to-day that
sheds his blood with me shall be my brother.

— William Shakespeare, *Henry V*

$\mathscr{B}$oys' schools, for good reason, are fond of Shakespeare's famous phrase
"band of brothers." We often cite it when we teach the concept of brotherhood. All of us, we preach, men and women alike, should strive to create
communities of fellow feeling, unity, and mutual assistance. At boys' schools
we begin at home, with brothers predominately like ourselves, and then like
expanding concentric circles, we strive to move farther afield into a world
always in need of brotherhood.

Shakespeare never lets good concepts play sentimental. In the Henry
plays, Prince Hal begins very much the adolescent boy with his own band of
brothers. Their bonds, however, are thievery, booze, and loose women; they
swear allegiance to each other but fake a robbery to humiliate their bloated
and whoring leader, the braggart Falstaff, whose mastery of language and wit
so entertains us that we forgive these drunks as if they were Robin Hoods
defending the poor instead of greedy, growing boys, always willing to betray
each other for personal gain.

We also forgive them because we know the irony of Hal's presence among
them. Of course they want to use the Prince. He—the most highly privileged
among them—is also using them to escape the responsibilities of growing up,
especially with a father who himself, using words that waxed sentimental, stole
the English crown from Richard II. Two plays later, we become inspired by the
young Prince Hal, grown now into Henry V, who when he rallies his under-
manned English troops at Agincourt, calls on them to be "a band of brothers."
And thus the phrase begins its journey to common usage.

14

We can't help remembering, however, all that has gone before as this handsome and powerful young leader risks his life and the lives of his men to take the crown of France. Throughout the plays, Falstaff argues that any deceit, whether in a pub or on the throne, is acceptable if needed to survive and, according to his seductive lights, live life to its fullest—a lesson no headmaster, however tempted, will endorse. I certainly don't argue against the supreme value of life but would prefer our boys choosing bands of brothers carefully. The bonds that tie them must be the right ones and held up to hard scrutiny.

I am reminded of the Henry plays when some of our boys, in arguing about honor, allude to the phrase "band of brothers." I wish I could say that every boy calling up the phrase knew the literary allusion, but I think the phrase has passed into current usage more because of the 101st Airborne in World War II than because of Shakespeare (not to say those paratroopers don't truly inspire us). But at St. Albans we debate, in chapel and in council meetings, the place of loyalty in a hierarchy of moral values. Not surprising, the issues are the same Shakespeare dramatizes.

Our boys understand the loyalty implicit in brotherhood ("because we are brothers I've got your back"). We, of course, encourage such loyalty as it pertains to supporting a fellow during hard times, whether it be as ultimately insignificant as his missing a foul shot that gives the victory to an opponent, or as ultimately significant as losing a parent in middle age to cancer. The boys face the temptation, however, of elevating this strong and important sense of loyalty over other moral values: loyalty over truthfulness, loyalty over honesty, and loyalty over integrity ("I've got your back even if we lie, cheat, or steal"). In other words, they can be seduced into being no more than young thieves in an Elizabethan pub. They excuse their thievery because of their distaste for adult authority and its obvious hypocrisies, their fear of growing up and having to take unpopular positions for moral reasons, and their sense of security in being part of a group of supposedly like-minded rebels and friends. They are often led by a kind of Falstaff among them, either the one most talented at language, most ready to use brute force to intimidate, or most gifted at psychological blackmail ("You know I've done something wrong, but you won't let anyone know because you don't want to be a rat").

Our tasks as teaching adults is to model how to choose more significant virtues over the virtue of loyalty—not simply truthfulness, honesty, and integrity, but justice, courage (including courage to confront a friend who steals), and love (not doll-eyed sentiment but rather love that brazens out the sin but loves the sinner). Loyalty can be misguided. Boys need to learn this. All their lives their friends, their lovers, their bosses, and their political leaders will call on them above all to be loyal.

It's a fine idea, up to a point.

Eighth Grade

I went to grade school when grammar ruled. On the English exam in January, the first page of questions required us to write the part of speech above each word in the sentence. Those directions seemed rather suspect to me. I thought writing "noun," "verb," "preposition," and so on for an entire page was too easy, was perhaps some kind of teacher's trick. I knew one fact for certain—this English teacher, this monster to rival Grendel's mother, didn't give gifts. So instead of writing "noun," I wrote the abbreviations for "subject," "direct object," "predicative nominative," or "object of the preposition." While in all cases except for the verbals, my syntactical answers were indeed the parts of speech we label "nouns," the teacher counted every answer wrong. Completely wrong—half credit was for the weak of brain.

The directions had asked for parts of speech, and I didn't follow the directions. I failed the exam with a thirty-five. In those days (1962), the exam was weighted so heavily—about 50 percent of the semester—that my term average fell to a 50. Also in those days, you received your grade by walking down the hallway to the classroom door, where the teacher posted a list of the students with their grades beside their names, for all the world and the world's cousins twice removed to see. Every classmate, and every freeloader, saw that I failed my first semester of English as an eighth grader.

This academic disaster led to others, of course. I barely passed calculus my senior year and was a falling body myself, lost in an apparent chaos of logarithmic tangents. In college, my freshman French teacher despised my southern accent. Every time I tried to respond in French, he mimicked my words back to me in some misguided effort to help me hear how I sounded. It humiliated me, didn't teach me French, and made me hate him to this day. In graduate school, the most distinguished critic of modernism then alive drew a line across the third page of my essay and wrote, "I can't read any more of this drivel."

I focus on the eighth-grade English exam, however, because it was the first blow. I can still remember in my stomach the door to my bedroom opening the night my grades arrived home. My father was, to all appearances, a gentle man. He walked into my bedroom and pulled up a chair next to my desk and said, in an almost unearthly and calm voice, that he and Mother weren't spending their hard-earned money to send me to a private school, which was unheard of in our families, so that I could come home with a grade like that. Arguing the finer points of either my grammatical misunderstandings—"But Dad, don't you see, I know what a part of speech is"—or my teacher's unfairness—"But Dad, he could have given me a retest"—would not wash. Every time my father thought of the word *virtue*, he saw it with a capital *V*. A teacher was Virtue with a capital *V*; his son's grade was Failure. If I did not shape up, I would go back to the public school whence I came, and in that typically post–World War II way of looking at things, he said that if I didn't get my act together by then, I could look forward to a life of digging ditches. He would still expect me to dig ditches well.

If Dad were alive now, he would smile—how we loved each other—and see me as a success and not a failure, even though I would tell him I spend a good portion of my days digging ditches of a different sort than he imagined. The point of the story, however, is that I survived the experience of walking down the hallway toward the posted grades and having a supposed friend of mine who saw them first—he was in fact a rival—look at me with contempt and say, "Wilson, you flunked English, you idiot!"

I've had a much harder time surviving this next story. It too was a blow I haven't forgotten. The first story has to do with my mind; the second, with my soul. In eighth grade we took what was called Old Testament, not as we would say today, the Hebrew Bible (I went to an Episcopal school from seventh to twelfth grades). I will not speak at length about the kind of family I grew up in or the generations that preceded me. But you can't understand the humiliation without my explaining that my mother's brother was named after William Jennings Bryan, the failed presidential candidate who prosecuted Mr. Scopes in the famous Monkey trials in Tennessee, against the defense attorney Mr. Clarence Darrow, hero of the play *Inherit the Wind*. My family, in other words, refused to admit that we might be descended from apes.

The first day of Bible class in eighth grade the teacher began by saying, "Surely there's no one in here who believes in the truth of the Adam and Eve story. If there is, raise your hand." Notice that the teacher didn't say "the literal truth of the Adam and Eve story." In those days, where I grew up, what he meant was "literal truth." To this day I am bruised by the story.

I was aware that I didn't come from an intellectual family, the kind that accepted Darwin's work when Teddy Roosevelt was the president. I also knew the sacrifices they were making to send me to a school that promoted intellectualism, but I am certain they saw education first as a way to get ahead in the world, not necessarily to improve on your belief system. My Bible teacher more than likely didn't know my background, but he knew enough about the culture of the time to ask the question. I firmly believe that the question itself is proof enough that he should not have used the tone he did, with the dripping arrogance in his use of "surely."

In and outside of the Christian church today, you will hear the phrase "Jesus blush." People use this phrase for many different reasons, most of them not very positive. It implies that Christians, people whose creed says "We believe in one Lord, Jesus Christ, the only Son of God," are nevertheless embarrassed by any discussion of Jesus at all and thus blush when his name is said. In other words, if some intellectual snob said, "Surely there is no one here in this school who believes Jesus Christ is the Son of God," we wouldn't have the courage to raise our hands. Fundamentalists and charismatics have usurped the name of Jesus, and Christians who are not fundamentalists and charismatics still haven't figured out how to speak about Jesus in these days of interfaith services and ecumenical movements and the embarrassment of missionary zeal among intellectuals.

Eighth grade was a tough year. I flunked English. I failed to raise my hand for a religious belief, a belief I no longer hold (while no one could believe more deeply in the truth of the Adam and Eve story, I know it isn't literally true). With this in mind, I encourage you never to brook someone else's efforts to humiliate you, whether for a poor academic performance or, more important, for a belief you hold. You should always try to improve a poor academic performance. You should always examine your beliefs, which will surely modulate and even change with every reexamination. Each of us has within our precious body a mind and a soul—they are who we are (body, mind, and soul). They are far more precious than money and fame and good looks, and caring for them is worth far more than any humiliation from the hurtful words of other people.

II

PARENTING

· 6 ·

A Boy's Voice

$\mathcal{A}$n essential concept a fledgling writer needs to understand and seek to master is voice. Most simply, *voice* is the idiosyncratic way an artist puts words together—why William Faulkner doesn't sound like Richard Wright and Maya Angelou doesn't sound like Louise Glück. A great artist strives in poetry or prose to be so distinctive as to be recognized prior to being named.

Good teachers of writing ask students to imitate famous voices—write a sonnet about the woods in the manner of Robert Frost; describe a railroad station where a Hemingway story takes place or an oppressive drawing room in an Edith Wharton story. In a slow, nonlinear, and at times despairing way, good students mature through imitation into a voice they can claim as their own.

At first our sons imitate us—a father's stride, a mother's laugh, a way of speaking. In time they seek their own voice—perhaps at first a strange blend of parents, but then distinctive. We should help them do this, not stand in their way, not continue to demand, consciously or not, they become a miniature us. Also, while we should demand of them moral behavior and that they become good men, they should not feel they must become the lawyer or the prince, the doctor or the preacher or the financial analyst we desire them to be, but who they themselves are. Their idiosyncratic "voice" is what we mean by vocation—an inner call, not only to find what Frederick Buechner labels our "deep gladness," but also how that gladness best meets the world's "deep need."

Most of us assume we do this. All too well we know parts of ourselves we don't want inherited or imitated. Carl Jung wrote that "if there is anything we wish to change in a child, we should first examine it and see whether it is not something that could be better changed in ourselves."

Still, we deceive ourselves and don't listen to our own good advice. We persist, sometimes thoughtlessly, sometimes in ways we later regret. Surely, we know them so well, we say to ourselves, better than anyone else who has come into their lives since birth, that only we know ultimately what is best for them. I am reminded of the folk saying, "The gods mock us by answering our prayers." Are all our prayers for our sons selfless? How many of us, then, think we were screwed up by our own parents' desires for us?

To help them discover a voice, we might rule out a great portion of talk about the future. We might not obsess over present-day accomplishments, no matter how spectacular. Instead we might concentrate on the quality of our day-to-day way of living—that's where we discover our voice, for to make the voice authentic, it needs to live in the warp and woof of the daily hours we keep. Flannery O'Connor, citing the Dutch priest and writer Henri Nouwen, calls this our "habit of being."

So let us model for our children certain habits. Show love, selflessly, and include in your love the necessary discipline for those who are shaping their own habits against pride and selfishness. Drive them crazy with how much you appreciate the lives we've been given—not the cheap ribbons given out for participation but the results of hard work or the serendipity of sudden beauty. Be a giver. Demonstrate serving, not simply your own family, but especially those in need. No child forgets working in a soup kitchen or steering the homeless or sitting in a convalescence home beside a sickbed. Be thoughtful. Show them that you, too, study; talk about what you're reading, also, or how you have a difficult problem at work to think through. And as difficult as your work might be, let them know why you do it and what you love about it.

But to return to where we started, you do this not to make our sons carbon copies, but to give them the model that will deepen their own distinctive voices, making their sounds resonant in new and creative ways that you will marvel at. That will be deep gladness.

· 7 ·

The Hours

When I was in my twenties and in my first teaching job in Atlanta, I spent some weekends at a nearby Trappist monastery. Before you assume anything meritorious about my religious life, my weekend pilgrimages were all about literature. I had befriended a Georgia State professor named Bill Sessions, who as a young man had made his pilgrimage to Milledgeville, Georgia, to befriend the Roman Catholic American writer Flannery O'Connor. O'Connor's stories wrapped their hands around my particular guts and squeezed them painfully dry. Bill invited me to the monastery to see Flannery's famous peacocks, which she had gifted to the monks in her will. Bill also introduced me to my favorite monk, Father Paul, Flannery's confessor and the brother who buried her. Father Paul, it turns out, had spent his pre-monastic youth in London and Paris, where he had befriended T. S. Eliot and James Joyce. Long story short, about literature, I was idolatrous: even to the point of spending weekends in a monastery's guesthouse.

Spiritual Lesson #1: Pray God we note the unforeseen.

Let me explain. I imagined myself, from a laughable and misplaced ambition, but one common to the young, as Flannery O'Connor's successor. Yet, I started to find the monastic life fascinating, with the one exception anyone can guess. But gathering together to pray at the same set hours every day, keeping silence together, sitting down to meals at three appointed times, in the afternoons working in the fields or baking bread or making jam or running errands and at appointed hours reading and studying: This routine felt calming to my soul and, potentially, immensely productive. I understand, in the world as we know it, the irony of calling monks who pray most of the day "productive."

23

But one reason I love our school is its traditions, which is primarily the repetition of an event at the same time in the year, the way a church calendar works its way through the same seasons and same biblical events each year, and our daily routine centered around being at a certain place at a certain time and, crucially, gathering together each day over food with an opening and closing prayer. You know I'm in the right business if I sing praises of a school schedule.

Fast forward thirty-five years. The diocese of Washington has a new bishop, a Minnesotan named Mariann Budde, who also serves as the head of our Protestant Episcopal Cathedral Foundation, of which our school and the Washington National Cathedral are a part. At our first trustees meeting, she gifts us John McQuiston's *Always We Begin Again: The Benedictine Way of Living*, a twentieth-century interpretation of the monastic rule established by a sixth-century Italian holy man, Benedict of Nursia. To begin the trustee meeting (yes, this is absolutely true), we read aloud together the book's passage on leadership.

Spiritual Lesson #2: Pray God, when given a gift by someone you respect, believe it comes like a visitation and make the most of it. Especially when the giver happens to be your bishop.

I have read this little Benedictine book twice and given it to my own friends. As I read, it plucks memories of my youthful need for order and routine and the safety of a cloister, whether it be my bedroom with a closed door or lying between two gables on our roof, where I would escape to stare into the night sky. As an adult, I feel the human kindness and divine inspiration pour from its words. And as a head of school, it inspires me to show our sons and daughters its wisdom while they grow up in a society thinking a cloister is an icon on a video game. I believe many of them, without even realizing the desire, ache for something like a daily Benedictine rule.

Every child—indeed every person—needs a cloister, however small or large: a nurturing enclosure that feels warm and safe. Human need begins with food and shelter. Every child needs the cloister also as an idea. It speaks of spiritual nurture, time to pray and work and rest, the trinity of a spiritual life. It speaks of a community with common cause. *It is best*, Benedict writes, *to live one's life with the support of a community that shares right values.*

Here is our task: raising our children in a cloister of right values. Be assured that the world they leave our cloister for will challenge those values.

Choose your own set of "family values." Benedict suggests these: to do good works, to teach and to learn, to forget ourselves, to keep silence, to take meals and to worship together, and when guests appear, to welcome them into the home and invite them into our routine. I hope as a school we can strive to model those same values here. Such ideals are, I know, a losing battle one day and a moment of grace the next.

I commend Benedict's rule for your study. For him, the rule begins with first principles, the moment we wake up, every single day. How wonderful it would be if this each day he describes could be ours:

> *At the beginning of each day, after we open our eyes to receive the light of that day, as we listen to the voices and sounds that surround us, we must resolve to treat each hour as the rarest of gifts. . . . Life will always provide matters for concern. Yet each day brings with it reasons for joy. Each day carries the potential to bring the experience of heaven; have the courage to expect good from it. Be gentle with this life, and use the light of life to live fully in your time.*

The Quality of Being There

The Irish say, when a child turns from its parents, that it is making strange.

—John Banville, *The Untouchable*

A senior I taught in the 1970s announced to his parents he was spending April and May in a tent he pitched in the backyard. He would come inside only to shower, change clothes, have his laundry done, and pick up some food on the go. Of course the food was to be prepared for him. Take that, Mom and Dad. I think he might have won a battle or two that spring but not the war. Still, I haven't forgotten.

In the 1980s I taught a senior whose mother started crying over their separation three months before graduation. I am not kidding. She visited school often—too often—and every time I saw her by myself or in a crowd of people, she was tearing up. Her daughter avoided her at all costs.

Consider how often each spring we hear the word "separation." It's the currency of parents, teachers, graduation speakers, psychologists, and columnists. Everyone barters its anxiety. I will return to these examples but want to flip the coin. Perhaps the opposite of "separation anxiety" might be the "joy of togetherness."

Apparently our wordsmiths coined the phrase "quality time" in the 1970s, when I started teaching. For all sorts of economic and social reasons, in the United States we decided that bursts of time with our children would suffice for good parenting. We did not need to be a parent present at the dinner table five nights a week but could spend three absolutely incredible spring days taking them to swim with the dolphins and barreling with them down Mount Something or Other. The quality of that close encounter of a secondary kind would nevertheless ground the parent-child relationship in the same way, perhaps even better, than the previous generation's "quantity of time," a poor phrase I create to make the point.

It is a fallacy to believe we can will "quality time" to happen. In fact it is a fallacy to think we can control time at all. We can create works of quality, of course, from a hand-crafted wooden toy to *Love in the Time of Cholera*, and we can make lists of all things that make our children happy, but no matter how hard we try, we do not have the supernatural power to infuse present experience with "quality." Present experience is also dull and routine, even in our marvelous and creative parental presence.

Most of us are not quietists, however, simply accepting the experiences life happens to offer. We travel to exotic places with the children or eat at their favorite restaurants or buy seats to professional games because these experiences often give them great pleasure and us time to sit side by side and soak in the spectacle and the conversation. But sometimes, not. There's no guarantee the Dude Ranch will work, the game won't bore them, or they'll throw a hissy fit when you make them put away their phones. Other times we try an opposite tact, believing as I do that a simple life will accomplish more—a "stay-cation." We even deny ourselves pleasure to give it a go. But whichever methods we choose and however hard we try, sometimes life is simply dry. Sometimes time doesn't cooperate with our plans.

In his book *The Call of Stories*, the moralist, essayist, and child psychiatrist Robert Coles describes going to bed upstairs in his house while his parents were together downstairs. We could mistake the scene for "nothing happening—no quality at all." Yet, Coles was aware that his parents were downstairs, together. As he fell asleep, he heard them talking to each other and sometimes even reading to each other. (They were devotees of George Eliot.)

I am aware of the demands on current parenting, on the economic necessities of global travel and long work hours (though a lot of other equally successful countries might disagree with the benefit of long work hours). My argument is that the young Robert Coles's simple awareness counts for a lot more than we choose to credit today—there is an adult presence in the house, one that needs to feel constant until the separation takes place at the end of senior year and everyone must live through the loss. Today, the presence of adults and children in the house together is complicated by our appetite for television and computers and iPhones, but I nevertheless think that simple presence—the quality of "being there"—nurtures our souls in ways that intense bursts of consciously manipulated "quality time" might or might not. And, when senior spring comes, with some weird behavior from our graduates unwilling to admit how scared they are, and tears waiting behind the curtains of our eyes, we will find that one way to deal with separation anxiety is to remind ourselves that, if nothing else, we have been present in our children's lives, and that's saying a good bit.

· 9 ·

Too Much of a Good Thing

$\mathcal{T}$he easiest way to kill a houseplant is to overwater it. A plant creates a gradient that attracts water into its root. To shift the ions necessary to create this gradient, a plant's cells produce energy by respiration, which requires oxygen. If we overwater a plant, the water fills up the vital air pockets around the roots and thus decreases soil oxygen, which keeps the plant from absorbing water. Or, as the ancient Mariner lamented, "Water, water every where . . . / Nor any drop to drink."

"All things are poison," Paracelsus writes, "and nothing is without poison. Only the dose makes the thing not a poison." It's not simply that we suffer if we don't get enough of a necessary chemical. We can also get too much of a good thing. Higher-than-appropriate doses of multivitamin and mineral supplements, for example, can result in toxicity. Another example is the fat-soluble vitamins A and D that we find in milk. If taken as additional supplements, they can also be toxic. On the other end of the scale, even selenium, a deadly poison at high doses, is physiologically necessary at very low doses. Just enough of a bad thing, so to speak.

All of us as parents pour good things into our children's lives. But could we be drowning them—keeping them from being able to breathe, to grow? This question doesn't test me too hard if I restrict my thinking as a parent to the rather obvious examples of material things. An excessively large room and house to grow up in might make a child's sense of scale too difficult to adjust when in his twenties he begins to live on his own and make judgments about how much space he needs and can truly afford. Giving a young boy too many toys—from hand-held games to gargantuan cars—devalues those toys. It can also stunt his ability to appreciate. Satisfying his every whim for a new technology might only thicken the walls around his psyche. He needs to grow up in the face-to-face world of human emotion.

28

However, I find that this question (are we drowning them—keeping them from being able to breathe, to grow?) is much more difficult to contemplate if I move beyond these easy questions about the material life. What if the good we are drowning them with is ourselves? What if the good is what we see as our precious love?

Fifty years ago, Canon Charles Martin, headmaster of St. Albans from 1949 to 1977, wrote a letter titled "The Process of Growth." In it he writes not simply about children growing up, but about our growth as parents. We too easily forget that we as parents are also called to grow.

Canon Martin's central example comes not from the world of botany but, not surprising, from animal life. As a young man he loved his purebred cocker spaniel (bulldogs came later). He loved the dog so much that he wanted to give it all the comforts of a dog's life and teach it to perform as many spectacular tricks as possible. He worked countless hours training the dog to show off his perfection, but instead of succeeding to teach the dog more tricks than any other spaniel could do, he literally drove the dog to distraction. He doesn't say in the letter which family or friends intervened, but he admits that the dog actually had to be taken away from him because he had almost killed it.

I borrow Canon Martin's parable because it is not about spoiling a child with material things. It asks us to question whether our overwhelming desire to help our children reach success, out of what feels like the best of intentions and even love, can become for them, when translated into action, poison.

Let us ask ourselves some simple questions. Are we allowing our children to grow into their own intellectual lives? Or are we doing their work for them, managing their schedules, demanding success? Each supportive decision about academics I make in isolation seems fine, but then my children take it upon themselves to remind me how heavy the cumulative effect of my "support" feels.

Are we encouraging an artistic life? Or are all those lessons, the extra rehearsals, the Hollywood demands turning us into the worst kind of "stage mothers"?

Is athletics a learning experience, a way to work hard with a high-performing group, and a road to good health? Or is athletics, for us, the ticket to our child's success, and thus we do all in our power, at whatever cost, to make our child into what we believe is a recruited athlete? And even so, to what end?

Dear friends, let us provide a learning environment at home by being learners ourselves. Let us model a moral life. Let us teach how to appreciate art by doing so. Let us keep ourselves healthy. And most of all, let us listen deeply to what our children are telling us. This is how we grow as parents, and if we grow in a healthy way, so will our children.

· *10* ·

Let the Rumpus Begin

"Now stop!" Max said and sent the wild things off to bed without their supper. And Max the king of all wild things was lonely and wanted to be where someone loved him best of all. Then all around from far away across the world he smelled good things to eat so he gave up being king of where the wild things are.

—Maurice Sendak, *Where the Wild Things Are*

*I*magine a group of adults gathered around a table.

On the table, a stack of books: Jane Austen, *Emma;* Donald Kagan, *The Peloponnesian War;* Maurice Sendak, *Where the Wild Things Are;* Elizabeth Gilbert, *Eat, Pray, Love;* the *Guinness World Records.* Then objects: a squishy ball, a Global Positioning System, a little shiny electric car that bumps around the table. Soon, I predict, you would be engaged. You might even be laughing about each individual's response to these things:

"You actually read the Guinness book of world records?"

"Don't you find Maurice Sendak a little dark?"

"My husband refuses to ask directions. I just rely on my GPS."

Perhaps the talk would turn, as these comments might be headed, toward gender differences.

I make two simple points, both apparently obvious: Boys and girls learn in different ways (which does not mean they don't share commonalities). Boys' behavior is normal.

You might assume I need not say that boys and girls learn in different ways. Or you might assume that as a head of a single-sex school I say so defensively. Thirty years ago, we were admonished that boys and girls were not to be treated differently but the same. The flags flown during this essential debate read "equality" and "equity." Many universities turned coeducational.

Single-sex schools went from being the rule to the exception. Now, in this country single-sex education has returned to fashion, especially in the charter and public realm, but in an effort "to rescue" boys from their dropping scores on standardized tests we must not lose the gains we made for the sake of girls. We say boys and girls learn differently only because we want to teach each gender most effectively and not at the expense of the other (this can be done in both single-sex and coeducational environments). But mark this history lesson. A hundred years ago, St. Albans was founded as a boys' school for cultural reasons. For it to be a boys' school now, it must be so for educational reasons.

Please note that a part of me bridles when I speak of gender differences, believing that all of us, whether male or female, live on a continuum. This is a current and fashionable thought but I accept it. Most important, we teach individuals first, but gender, class, race, and culture are crucial aspects of a person's individual identity.

Here are some challenging examples, and only a few, of how, in the classroom, boys and girls are different:

The average girl reads better than the average boy into early secondary school. The average young girl's vision has better perceptual speed up close than the average boy's, and she is thus better at picking out specific items in an array of items, a talent which of course helps her in reading. The average boy's vision tends to involve quick eye movement—he doesn't like staying focused on a face. His focus is most often on things that move and on distance, giving him, along with his right-side brain development, strong spatial skills. Imaging research into memory, a key component to learning, shows that males use visual strategies to remember, while females use verbal strategies. Thus boys tend to learn better when they see the information depicted pictorially and they can literally interact with the information, especially if they can use their hands and bodies in their learning. Girls remember well from an auditory source. Tell them, they will talk about it, and they will remember. At the age of one, given the choice, girls looked longer at videos of other people's faces while boys looked longer at videos of moving cars.

Just as you might assume I need not say that boys and girls learn differently, you might also assume I don't need to say that boy behavior is normal. But many people, including, most significantly, teachers, perhaps unconsciously, think "average" girl behavior is normal while "average" boy behavior is suspect. I speak from experience. Before coming to St. Albans, I taught at a very fine girls' school in Baltimore, the Bryn Mawr School. I remember spending a day in classes full of hard-working, articulate, homework-completing, and in some cases teacher-pleasing girls only to have the boys from Gilman School across the street, in our tri-school relationship, arrive for my afternoon coordinate class, bringing with them their oversized, slouching bodies; their loudness, rowdiness, and incomplete homework; their efforts at rudeness until squelched; and their preening male egos. I had to catch myself before I decided that these guys were suspect. The truth was, they were normal. They were yours truly, age sixteen.

Consider the story of Max, who, author Maurice Sendak tells us, "wore his wolf suit and made mischief of one kind and another." "His mother called him 'WILD THING!' and Max said 'I'LL EAT YOU UP!' so he was sent to bed without eating anything." In a mere 338 words, Sendak recounts how Max's room transformed into a forest beside an ocean. Max sailed off to the land where the wild things "roared their terrible roars and gnashed their terrible teeth and rolled their terrible eyes and showed their terrible claws"—until Max told them "BE STILL!" and tamed them by staring into their eyes. After leading the wild things in a rumpus, Max sent them all to bed without supper and sailed home, where he found supper waiting for him—"and it was still hot."

How do we as teachers of boys, and as parents of sons, understand this archetypal story? How do we walk with our wild things, with their slowly developing prefrontal lobes and their preference for fast cars over faces, with boys who learn in different ways from girls but *are* who they *are*? How do we walk with them so that when given a choice, as Max is, of being king of the wild things or being loved best of all, our sons choose love? They sit down to a hot meal.

This is how.

Look a boy in the eye and call him by name. You are Max the wild thing. I am Vance the headmaster. You are Max my son. I am your father. Give him not a wild day, but a structured day in which wildness is scheduled. Call his name each hour. Solve this problem, Max. Translate this passage, move your adverb next to the word it modifies, Max. I appreciate your telling the truth, Max. Show up on time. Do not hit in here, Wild Thing, there is plenty of time for rumpuses on the playing field. At home Max will explode—slam the door, speak disrespectfully, and beat on a sibling. Give him some time, some space, but call him out. Max, set the table. Let's see your homework. Leave your little sister alone—don't you realize what she's busy doing? Put his cell phone on the mantle before he goes to bed. Don't answer your cell when you're talking to him.

Fill his life with stories and with rituals. Sit in chapel, Max, listen to the silence, sing, and reflect on what your classmates say. Sit down to lunch with us. Let me tell you some stories about the names on these walls. And I'm an English teacher. Have you read the story about those choir boys turned savages? How could that have happened? You know this Mr. Knightley character in Jane Austen? What do you think of him?

Tell him so many family stories and take him to so many family events that he rolls his eyes constantly for four to six years. In your family stories, forget the morals; tell the stories. If the story is worth telling, he will remember it. Make him feel part of the tribe.

Finally, model. Boys learn from how we live our lives in front of them. We must be empathetic, challenging, fair, positive, strict, and human. Psychologist and author Michael Thompson gives great advice to mothers and fathers. He asks mothers to spend some time thinking about a man they deeply admire: Of course it could be their husbands, but it might also be a father, a grandfather, an uncle, or simply a friend. Find a photograph of that man and put it somewhere in the house. When you discover that Max is up to things you cannot believe, when Max goes public with a rumpus, or simply when Max seems unable to get his act together, look at that photograph. Max will get there. I promise you. Give him time.

And fathers. No single person "made you into a man." It's a dangerous phrase. You made yourself into a man, and if you're anything like me, you're still apprenticing. Remember your vulnerabilities. If your mother is still alive, you might talk to her about them. She will remember. Nothing has profited me more as a father than to recall just how deeply emotional adolescence is. The highs and lows. Remember how the minor offense became major. How young love burned a hole in your lungs. How disappointment seemed irreparable. Fathers, find the rituals that mean something to you and do them with your sons. Forget the moralizing as part of it. Just be there, a steady emotional presence at your son's side.

In the end Max the Wild Thing calls us to our ministries. My colleagues and I on the faculty are called to teach the young. No vocation is more sacred. Mothers and fathers have been blessed with children. However trying those children can be, they *are* a blessing. Let us together, teachers and mothers and fathers, walk with these children through the primal sin of disobedience and through the rumpuses of adolescence until we sit down together again with our grown children and share a hot meal.

· 11 ·

On Specialization

*W*ithout question, Jeffrey Wright, a 1983 graduate of St. Albans, is a star—honored with Tony, Drama Desk, and Outer Critics Circle awards. When at St. Albans, Jeffrey was not an actor. Others would fault this school—how could you blithering idiots not recognize his talent?—but I don't fault us at all. While here, Jeffrey excelled—but at his studies, lacrosse, journalism, and photography. He didn't try out for his first play until his junior year at Amherst, and the way Jeffrey tells the story, he auditioned only to win a bet with a roommate.

Jonathan Ogden, St. Albans class of 1992, is also a star—a first-round selection to the NFL Hall of Fame, a career as All-Pro Offensive Tackle with the Super Bowl champion Baltimore Ravens, an honors history graduate from UCLA, and the funder of a foundation devoted to the children of Baltimore. Jonathan led us to many football victories, but he was also a three-sport athlete and fine student. I must correct myself. He wrestled until he was a sophomore and wanted to continue, but the league declared him ineligible because he was heavier than the heaviest weight allowed for the heavyweight category. He was thus banished to the weight room. He still holds our track records for the shot-put and discus, having once thrown the discus over the fence at the far end of the Sidwell Friends' track and into the window of an unsuspecting and innocent and fortunately unoccupied car.

Dreaming of the Olympics, Jonathan had a modest request for college recruiters: In addition to playing football, he wanted to throw the shot. With the exception of two coaches, the recruiters told Jonathan he would have to forget track and field and specialize year-round in football. In 1994 and 1995 at UCLA, Jonathan finished fifth in the NCAA's indoor shot-put event, and in 1995 he finished fourth in the outdoors with a heave of 61'1½". The next year he won the indoor competition with a throw of 63'9". For those of you who don't know track, these are world-class tosses.

And may I reiterate? He was an honors history graduate.

All of us know that the path these two superstars took would today appear foolish. We are raising a generation of children who believe that the only way to become a star is to begin soon after birth and specialize. Pardon my hyperbole, but if Jeffrey and Jonathan were our generic sons, I'm afraid as parents we'd be so astute about their genius that we'd send Jeffrey to "quarterback camp" and Jonathan to "acting camp." Yes, there's a touch of the cynic in that statement, but my point is intended to be helpful.

For what I believe is best for our children is slow growth. Our culture devalues free time, overemphasizes speed, and chews up celebrities by the week. Mastodon that I am, I am still wed to supposedly outdated ideas of a classical education. Such an education is founded on the experience of history, on the liberal arts, on skills that will be transferable among the three or four careers each of our children might pursue as they work into their seventies, and on the creaky idea of distributional requirements that keep young people at work on different kinds of intellectual disciplines as late as their sophomore year in college. How many of our aspirations for our own child come from our sense that our own life's dreams are being reworked, some even abandoned, each passing year? As a father, I have often had to remind myself to grow up.

In his autobiography, John Stuart Mill tells the story of his father James's rigorous efforts to shape him from childhood into a highly educated and ardent Benthamite. The father's specialized regimen gave the boy little time for anything but house study and daily walks with his father, during which time the senior Mill would lecture his son on the principle of utility or question him about his studies and beliefs. James Mill succeeded, in a way. At age eight, his son had read Herodotus's *Histories* in the original Greek. Before his son turned twenty, the young man founded the original Utilitarian Society, led a clique of students called "The Philosophical Radicals," and helped to found *The Westminster Review*. But at the age of twenty, John Stuart Mill had a severe nervous breakdown.

James Mill has been passed down to us, probably unfairly, as a quintessentially bad Victorian father—highly demanding, emotionally distant, and wed to reason and accomplishment at all costs. He is seen as the cause of his son's mental health crisis. Some critics even argue that his son's relationship with his father led to John Stuart Mill's most sustaining adult belief—in effect a kind of anti-belief. John Stuart Mill eventually believed that "the pursuit of happiness" needs to derive not only from reason and a principle of utility, as his father had taught him, but also from a cultivation of feelings, from a wide-ranging exposure to music, art, and poetry, and, most particularly, from friendship—in other words, what was missing in his childhood.

This is a complex example, for much of the senior John Mill's regimen derived from the classical education I believe in, only he tailored it to convert his son to his own cause and gave his son no time on his own or for what in today's parlance we call "free play." He stuffed his parenting down his son's throat.

What will our offspring say about their childhood years when they write their own autobiographies?

III

LOOKING INWARD

The Spiritual

· 12 ·

An Eternal Present

Let anyone try, I will not say to arrest, but to notice or attend to, the present moment of time. One of the most baffling experiences occurs. Where is it, this present? It has melted in our grasp, fled ere we could touch it, gone in the instant of becoming.

—William James, *The Principles of Psychology*

In his book *Flow*, Mihaly Csikszentmihalyi explains that in getting so fully immersed in an activity we might lose our self-consciousness—we don't think about either our "being" or our "becoming." All of us know the feeling: reading, exercising, watching a great play, lying on our backs beneath an autumn sky, we disappear from ourselves until we suddenly look at a clock. Time has passed, unknowing. As we self-consciously acknowledge the time ("hey, look how late it is"), the present "melts in our grasp" and disappears "in the instant of becoming." But if we lose our self-consciousness and do not try to mark the time, we exist in a "flow," what might feel, miraculously, at least as we surface into self-consciousness, as if we were in an eternal present. The flow is, ironically, simultaneously a stop in the marked tick-tock of time.

Apparently, this flow most frequently happens in activities with a clear set of goals, a balance between a perceived set of skills and the perceived difficulty of the task, and clear and immediate feedback that sustains the task. Let's take watching a great play for an example. I arrive in the theater with a clearly set goal to be entertained. My parents and teachers introduced that goal to me when I was young, and as an adult I have embraced its worth, to both enjoy and perhaps feel provoked by a play—provoked to think, disagree, or, best of all, to wonder. My parents and teachers helped me create a skill set I bring to the theater—a mind that can pay attention, eyes to observe, and an empathetic but critical inner sensibility. If the play doesn't require exercising my skill set, I grow bored with its clichéd plot, wooden dialogue, and false sentiment. But if the play challenges those skills and entertains me, I lose myself in a flow created by its beautiful making.

I check my watch. My goodness, I had no idea. Where did the time go?

And who are the personalities most prone to these conditions of flow?

Headmasters unfortunately don't make the list.

"The person," Csikszentmihalyi writes, "needs few material possessions, comfort, power, or fame because so much of what he or she does is already rewarding. Because such persons experience this so-called flow in work and family life, or when interacting with people, when eating, even when alone with nothing to do, they are less dependent on the external rewards. They are more autonomous. They are independent because they cannot be as easily manipulated with threats or rewards from the outside. At the same time, they are more involved with everything around them because they are fully immersed in the current of life." The philosopher commends missionaries and scientists as being particularly prone to this flow.

That feels like a set-up: Religion and Science, now bow to each other!

Nevertheless, these characteristics of those prone to flow, so to speak, belie what I label the U.S. Industry of Happiness and Greed. Self-help authors, Madison Avenue marketers, advertisers of all products under the sun, investment advisors, and consultants of all shapes and sizes, many of whom are in my experience very good and purposeful people, do not promote "[needing] few material possessions, comfort, power, or fame" as a recipe for happiness. They don't target "independent people . . . [not] easily manipulated with threats or rewards from the outside." At their standing worktables, they don't search for "autonomous people . . . fully immersed in the current of life," that is, if the autonomy means a disregard for buying a thing.

Csikszentmihalyi's research raises crucial questions about the art of living. Is this so-called flow worth accepting as real and possible, even working toward as a goal, helping myself, sorting and resorting my life to make what sounds nearly blissful happen? In truth it feels like hard work, even of the spiritual kind, as if I need to retreat to a desert to prepare.

And who can sustain that effort?

Isn't the alternative better? Pursue wealth, comfort, power, and fame and better become the person I think I want to be and the person much of the world will admire?

As a child I was taught the prevailing Hebraic sense of time—a pilgrim's progress through what we call history, with some of us chosen and some not, toward the end, when divine rewards are won according to the faith and works demonstrated in my all too sinful segment of life on that linear march.

"Flow" was understood, I believe, but seen as what we refer to as "grace," a god-like visitation that for a moment takes us out of straight lining toward death and gives us a revelation. "Grace" was never earned.

I believe in the essential value and even divinity of what I accept as "flow." Even as we apparently know in what circumstances it most frequently happens, I also believe that it is filled with aspects of the divine—an eternal present that the greatest missionary might feel in serving the Gospel and a true scientist in serving humankind. Thus we can work for it but also must wait for it, prayerfully.

We work for it as Csikszentmihalyi describes—without worrying about material possessions, comfort, fame, or power, and by keeping ourselves from being manipulated by threats or rewards from the outside. I think trying to make the flow itself happen will fail more often than not, but the preparation necessary for it to happen on its own is within our power.

Curse, then, the so-called Happiness Industry: It wants your money in order to make you try something that loses value almost immediately so that you return to try again. Think "shopping therapy."

Own what you need. Take comfort in your relationships. Serve others—there is power in that. Fame comes or it does not, and it never knocks on the door wearing the clothes you expected.

Some people will not like your direction. They will say you're falling behind your neighbors and social friends. You must be uncomfortable, in this phase you're going through, by your obvious weaknesses and insignificance. Read this other book, they advise. See this therapist. Buy this suit. Join this club. Hire the right designer. Invest in this fund and walk along the beach in white beachcomber pants and a denim shirt, with no one else in sight because you can afford it.

A very wise counselor in his eighties once told me that he thought of himself as an apprentice.

This sensibility I describe is idealistic, I realize. Let us apprentice at it. And that's enough.

• 13 •

The Prophet in His Own Homeland

$\mathcal{I}$ was born in Asheville, North Carolina, a small city that nevertheless serves as the most significant metropolis in the mountains of western North Carolina. It is to Washington, D.C., what Nazareth was to Jerusalem, an out-of-the-way place. Some provincial thinkers might ask about it, as the disciple Nathanael asked about Nazareth, "Can anything good come from Asheville?"

One of my strongest childhood memories is a dinner one July evening in the mid-1950s on the veranda of my grandparents' house. It was a perfect evening. The summer's heat was dying, as it did every night in the mountains; Grandmother and Mom had prepared a magnificent meal of fresh corn on the cob, pork chops, turnip greens, cole slaw, and blueberry pie with homemade ice cream on top; and all of us sat silently together at the end of the meal and watched the fireflies come out. My father sternly coached my brother and me to sit still until we were dismissed from the table, when we could run out into the yard and catch a firefly in our mason jars. What a mystery it was, that a little bug, here and then there, would light up like a miniature flying lantern!

My uncle Turk was in town this July evening, on leave from the Navy. I knew in a nonverbal way, in the way that only children know, that he was the wayward sheep of the family, the prodigal son. No one had ever explained why. But my grandparents were different when he visited—stiffer, more on guard, more likely to lecture—and inevitably, after a day or two, an argument would break out, tears would be shed, and my uncle would abruptly leave.

The argument usually focused on my uncle's way of living, which my grandparents disapproved of. But in a strange twist, this night my uncle made my grandfather livid because of the way someone else had lived decades earlier, in the 1920s. My uncle claimed that some man I didn't know was the greatest person in my grandparents' generation in Asheville. This unknown man was greater than the city's adopted son William Jennings Bryan, or the evangelist named Billy Sunday, and surely this young new evangelist named Billy Graham. By implication, of course, he was greater than my own grandparents.

Why adults could get so angry over such a stupid question I had no idea, especially with the prospects of a second piece of pie and all those fireflies in the yard. But my uncle said something like, "The rest of you are so dull, Father. Asheville finally produces a man the rest of the world can look up to, and your entire generation disowns him. You bring disgrace upon yourselves."

I thought my grandfather would bust. This infamous man was a disgrace to the community, my grandfather said. The man had no business airing out people's laundry in public and lying about it half the time. Making up lies. He never held a real job in his life and used his family for his own ends. Then my grandmother added that this man's sins were the worst kind of sins, for they had a terrible influence on the young. My brother and I were listening carefully by then. Besides that, the man was a drinker, and besides being a drinker, he had moved to New York City, and as everyone knows, what good can come from New York City?

The argument ended as most family arguments around a dinner table do. Someone cut more pie. Someone else changed the subject. The principals seethed in silence for a while. The kids were let free to play and provide a diversion. I didn't discover the identity of this terrible man they argued about until fifteen years later. No avid reader of novels who found out I was born in Asheville, North Carolina, could pass up the opportunity to ask what I thought of a writer named Thomas Wolfe. Thomas Wolfe is a novelist whose reputation has been on the decline for a while now and who is sometimes mistaken for the contemporary novelist Tom Wolfe. Thomas Wolfe's most famous book, an exposé of the Asheville society of my grandparents' generation, was called *Look Homeward, Angel.* His most famous title, which may end up being what he is best remembered for, alludes to the Gospel of Luke, chapter 4, in which Jesus preaches in Nazareth. "Is not this Joseph's son?" the astonished crowd asks. Jesus responds: "Truly, I tell you, no prophet is accepted in the prophet's hometown." Enraged, the crowd chases Jesus out of town and up a hill "so that they might hurl him off the cliff." Thomas Wolfe, rejected by at least some of his Asheville generation, entitled this last novel *You Can't Go Home Again.*

How quickly we, heroes in our own minds, identify with the outcast and the exile. We identify with Thomas Wolfe the brilliant novelist and not the dull, Babbitt-like citizens of Asheville. We identify with the prodigal son in the pigsty and not the virtuous elder brother who stayed at home. We identify with the Christ who can't go home again in Luke's gospel story. No one hasn't felt misunderstood by his or her family at least once, painfully so, and under-appreciated by neighbors and teachers and schoolmates. All of us have also delighted in being away from home and not identified as So-And-So's son or daughter and being judged only for ourselves and not our relation to family or kinsfolk or hometown. We believe, with Mark Twain, that our genius can't be discovered by our hometown because people are so close to us that our genius is out of focus. Or with Emerson, we say that our cousins can say nothing about us. And when most bitter, we say with Jonathan Swift, "When a true genius appears in the world, you may know him by this sign, that the dunces are all in a confederacy against him."

But let us be truthful. Might you not agree with me when I say we like to see ourselves as outsiders of genius? As heroes? But we are not. We are not the prophet and certainly not the savior. We are the disbelieving locals of Nazareth, the fault-finding citizens of Asheville. We are the neighbors of Joseph and Mary, the kinsfolk who work every day and go to church and do our fair share of gossiping. Aren't we the same ones who get up and drive Jesus out of the town so that we might hurl him off the cliff?

I cannot explain why we act this way, why we imagine ourselves one way and live another. We tend to find fault with the Jesus who lives next door instead of looking for something in him to praise. When the Jesus next door becomes part of our routine, we grow blind to him. Or we become jealous of his success. If the Jesus next door is merely a carpenter's son, we might be so prejudiced as to believe the divine can't arise out of our social and economic inferior, or out of someone from a different race from ours. And all the while we are quick to see how others persecute us and don't recognize our own worth.

What, then, can we do? How can we look up from the dinner table where we argue with each other over who is the greatest and instead see the fireflies burning in the yard, the little lanterns of light all around us? I can only say, my friends, pray unceasingly, whatever your understanding of praying is. Pray for grace, some mysterious infusing of a better self. And let us act on our prayers. Let us pray for truth-telling and tell the truth, pray for the ability to praise and then sing praises, pray for new eyes to see with and turn everyone's attention at the table to the fireflies in the yard, and pray for an end to our jealousies and prejudices and disappointments within our families. And what may happen? A lot more than fireflies: visitations of this grace. We may with Abraham have angels come into our tents; we might with Jacob wrestle an angel throughout the night; we may have our brother Joseph restored to us, or lie in bed and hear a still small voice calling our name; or most blessedly, be walking on the road to Emmaus only to discover we walk side by side with the resurrected Jesus, the same man who was our next-door neighbor, the one we once wanted to push off the edge of a cliff, and whom we now call Master.

· 14 ·

A Rough Coming

The first snowstorm of the season, and winter is thirteen days from arriving. It blows rough winds that roar around the west front of the cathedral and threaten to lift us, literally, off our feet. It dumps heavy snow. It dumps the flu. It piles up black slush. We rise in the dark and go to school; we work all day, sometimes in the faintest of light, and we go home in the dark.

Winter can be, for our spirits, a season of discontent. "Every mile is two in winter," said poet and priest George Herbert. Classes seem twice as long, bodies ache twice as intensely, tests feel twice as hard, and the distress of mind and soul and heart appear twice as threatening. During this season we begin on the shortest day of the year, December 21, and winter monsters come calling—their names are depression, self-pity, and despair. They knock all too often on the doors of our souls. For some of us, these monsters can become a disease as ferocious as cancer and can be cured only by therapy and medicine. But all of us, regardless, must deal with these monsters.

I offer you four spiritual exercises. Yes, "exercise" is a word you can use with "spirit"—there is a long history of linkage. We know how to exercise our minds and bodies, but we must also exercise our souls or, quite simply, our souls get fat, rot, and die. But as in all things, each exercise has a positive and a negative side.

The first I call "comparison shopping." Everyone knows what that is, especially this time of year. We look around until we find the best deal. A beginning spiritual exercise simply asks us to look around the world and compare our deal with other people's. Who has been given the most advantages? Who doesn't have to worry about the next meal, about freezing to death, about a warm place to sleep? I could document the overwhelming advantages given to those of us at St. Albans, but I think you know.

As I said, there are positives and negatives to each of these spiritual exercises.

The success of the first exercise depends upon the spirit we bring to it. If you are prideful, the exercise can reaffirm your pride and make you believe, just because you have material advantages, that you are better than those who have less. People who live in a desert of material goods might have richness in their hearts, and those of us who live in material luxury might have deserts in our hearts. Also, conversely, looking in the opposite way, if you are depressed and you approach any kind of comparison exercise with a negative consciousness, you will eventually be able to find someone better off than you are. He has more stuff, he makes better grades, he is a better athlete or actor, he is handsome, and I am not. Ninety-nine percent of the rest of the world has none of our collective advantages, and yet our dark negativism might focus only on the 1 percent where we fall short. The final disadvantage to this exercise is that it is primarily intellectual, and if sadness and depression attack the mind first and foremost, it's hard to talk ourselves out of them solely by the force of mental will. And yet there is a great positive to this exercise if you can muster the right spirit for it.

Many of us today are list-makers. The lists we make usually are the tasks we need to accomplish, and the purpose of making the lists is to ensure that we don't forget our assignments or errands and their deadlines. Make a list of assignments. Finish a task. Make the deadline. Draw a line through. Make another list tomorrow. A second spiritual exercise, arising out of the first, is list-making; the list is not the work you need to do but the blessings you have been given. The difference between this exercise and the first is that you are not thinking about your advantages in life—income and material goods—but about relationships: friends, family, teachers, and colleagues who mean a lot to you, who make you who you are, who help you find meaning in life and feel some kind of self-worth and satisfaction. Notice that the mental activity of the first exercise is not enough here. For this list, you need to feel inside what your blessings are.

In both the first book of *The Iliad* and the eighth book of *The Odyssey*, Homer tells us that laughter is a gift from the gods. Ancient literature also emphasizes how important it is in life to be hospitable—to open the door to your home, build a fire, share food, sit together, tell stories, and laugh together. This communion among people doesn't happen without working at it, and this is our third exercise.

Think about this maxim: He who laughs, lasts. The great comic writer Max Beerbohm said, "Strange, when you come to think of it, that of all the countless folk who have lived before our time on this planet not one is known in history or in legend as having died of laughter." Freud has taught us that the motivations behind laughter can be complex, and I acknowledge the negative side of laughter. Boys' schools are notorious for cruel humor; in fact, Australian-born writer Clive James said he learned to make people laugh only to protect himself from all the fun that was made of him when he was a boy in school. Nevertheless, we need to exercise our laughter together, and we need to build it around being hospitable to one another and telling stories together. If we sit down and eat and tell funny stories and laugh at our own foolishness and the sometime absurdity of life, nothing can better make us feel the light coming into the darkness. This last point is a transition into my final exercise, for one of the great theologians of the twentieth century, Reinhold Niebuhr, once wrote that "laughter is the beginning of prayer."

By prayer, as the fourth exercise, I mean being still, quiet, and listening. In December, especially for those of us who are Christians, we live in the most ironic time of the year. The season of Advent is a season of repentance and waiting for the visitation of the divine into the everyday, not as we expect to be visited, but in some kind of surprise—a baby born in a manger when we expect a powerful king, an innocent when we expect a warrior son of David. But the preparation not for the Savior but for Christmas instead—at St. Albans preparing for the final tests before vacation, rehearsing for lessons and carols, decorating for the house tour, shopping—is anything but a time of quiet waiting. I encourage you to understand that furious activity doesn't safeguard us against depression or despair. I encourage you, on the other hand, to know that quiet prayer doesn't guarantee happiness. But the exercise of the spirit—through mental comparisons of our existence with others, through listing our blessings, through laughter and storytelling, and through prayer—better prepares us for however God will come into our lives. God will come. He doesn't ask permission. He just comes. I cannot tell you how that will happen. I can assure you only one thing, and that is that you will be surprised.

· 15 ·

Silence

$\mathscr{I}$n the eighth century BC, the priests of India devised a competition to discover who or what God was. The first contestant asked an enigmatic question. For example: "If it is in the nature of God to reveal Himself, why is he inscrutable?" The opponent, a second contestant, was charged with answering by posing another enigmatic question. "If God is God, is God good? If God is good, is God not-God?" The contest continues, one side against another, amping up the inscrutability.

Pardon my crustiness, but if there were such a "discover God" contest today, twenty-nine centuries later, would it not be live-streamed, dumbed down, and full of spectacle? The producers would include a beautifully coiffed and suspicious master of ceremonies out of *The Hunger Games*; as the contestants prepared to speak, an undertone of suspenseful music would play; a rowdy crowd would cheer each side; and some electronic scoring system would emblazon the point total above the contestants' anguished faces on a Jumbotron.

But in the eighth century, the design of the contest intentionally reduced both sides to silence. The point was to realize no words would suffice.

Nearly every religion makes a similar point: As essential as speech is, especially the kind of speaking and writing we emphasize at our school, ultimately, words are impotent. In the face of mystery, the only human response left at a moment of revelation is silence.

On Mount Horeb, Elijah hears God's voice but only in the silence. Isaiah's suffering servant: He keeps silent, no matter how much he suffers. When Pilate and the priests question Jesus, he keeps silent. Apophatic theology is the study of what God is not. It is a keenly important branch of theology that C. S. Lewis argues in *Miracles* is the place to begin: simply,

48

what God is not. I believe the path to God includes the charge to season our thinking and our speaking and our daily living with silence, which in a way, is not-saying. Instead of mouthing off, swallow our words. Govern our speech. Restrain ourselves.

We come into chapel at least twice a week, gather ourselves, and hear the words, "The Lord is in His Holy Temple. Let all the world keep silence before Him," and for twenty-five to seventy seconds, depending upon the leader, we keep a sacred, gathering silence together until we must, as human creatures, try words of prayer to express our hearts. Contemporary culture hates silence. It despises silence. It tries to eliminate silence in your life, for silence might calm your breathing, cleanse your mind, and perhaps lead to choices that don't involve the speedy buying and selling of material goods. Think about it. Do we need cell phones on plane flights, or does the cell phone industry want to enslave you? Do we need our GPS devices in the middle of the Rocky Mountains, or do these devices disable you?

I could go on a very long time. Instead, I ask you to be thoughtful about the noise in your life. Perhaps you might consider tuning out, turning off, and saying no. Saying no might be the word of God.

· 16 ·

Rhythm

Keeping the Difficult Balance

> [In life] you just can't get away from rhythm. . . . The left hand shakes with the right hand, the inhale follows the exhale, the systole talks back to the diastole, the hands play patty cake, and feet dance with each other. And the seasons. And the stars, and all of that. And the tides, and all that junk. You got to live at peace with it, because if it's going to worry you, you'll lose.
>
> —Saul Bellow, *Henderson the Rain King*

Saul Bellow's passage impresses in its expansive physicality: from the body—hands that shake, lungs that breathe, a heart that beats, feet that dance; to the earth in the tides, followed by the sky in the seasons and stars, and all that. The passage helps us to nod agreement to emotional dyads: love, hate; body, soul; give, take; stop, go; yes, no. More than likely we also nod agreement to Bellow's last line: "You got to live at peace with it, because if it's going to worry you, you'll lose."

Implicit in that last line is my question: Why *don't* we live in peace with it? Why don't we say, "Hey, Life, there's a rhythm to you, and I win by accepting both sides; I wake, but I sleep—fine; I win, and sometimes lose—ok!; I work, but I also play—huzza!" Why struggle instead to be always awake, always winning, and always working? More crucial to our purposes as parents: Why don't we figure out ways to help our children accept the back-and-forth and live at peace with it, for if they worry about it, they'll lose. And their loss often hurts us more than our own failure.

I restate the problem. We flirt with becoming one-sided—all right-handed, all forward. We exert a willpower that never gives in, a need to control and never submit to another's wishes, an obsession over work and no rest, a low-grade guilt about not working and an inability to celebrate work as we do, a need for some kind of status and more money (there never seems to be enough money) in lieu of commonness and enough money, a concern never for our soul but always for our image (for no one in Washington is unaware of the image machinery we live with), a phenomenal ability to get work done and to generate more work to do, an obliviousness to the world around us, and intensity, intensity, intensity. Please pardon me if I have offended you. This pot calls the kettle black.

Remember the first time you saw a physical gesture of your child's that you recognized as your own? Maybe you didn't even see it, but your spouse or parent pointed it out to you. Our children grow up looking at us, literally, and then studying us. Increasingly they listen less to our words. The same is true in a school. We can preach at them three times a week or we can recite the school philosophy at the beginning of each class, but all of us know that students accept the rhythms of life if they watch us do so. They know whether our actions suit our words.

How, then, to live at peace with the back-and-forths? I love teaching Arthur Miller's *Death of a Salesman* because of the resonate leitmotif: *attention must be paid.* Attention deficit, we know, is a condition that can be helped medically. Focus can be helped by doing fewer things and by developing the ability to identify the most important task at hand. And our children more often than not, as they age, don't want our attention. I argue that nothing brings appreciation of the yin and yang of life like paying concentrated attention.

Accept that the rhythm cannot be changed. We cannot force life into one box of our making. Take grief as an example. All of us have suffered the loss of loved ones. "[T]o get born," Louise Glück writes, "your body makes a pact with death / and from that moment, all it tries to do is cheat." When our pact runs out, those of us who mourn can follow all the experts' advice of keeping to ritual, being open, meeting those who offer consolation. We can think ourselves done with it. But grief unawares can return six months later and shock us, scorning any sense we are masters of life.

Finally, praise. We get distracted so as not to pay attention, we argue rather than accept, and we criticize rather than praise. But we lift ourselves up in the act of praising. This is very hard to do on any consistent basis and very hard to teach adolescents, who because of their age in life naturally tend to tear down, not build up. As a young man, I thought praising others or God was dull. Excruciatingly dull. I was far more interested in forgetting God altogether, and if I couldn't do that, wrestling with God like Jacob—and winning. I certainly didn't want to bow down before him like Isaiah. However true the difference in demeanor is for young and old, we can set examples before our children by taking the time to praise God, to appreciate life, to praise our children but only when they deserve it, and to see the divine in the everyday.

I was delighted when Richard Wilbur's *Collected Poems* was published and critics acknowledged that the attention given his work from 1947 until now was much less than the attention given to equally great poets, but ones who had to jump off bridges in Minnesota, walk in front of cars in Chapel Hill, go in and out of mental hospitals in Boston, or stick their heads in ovens in London (John Berryman, Randall Jarrell, Robert Lowell, and Sylvia Plath). I don't mean to demean these poets' greatness or their suffering. Wilbur received less attention because his poetry is elegant, formal, and full of praise for life. It is not suicidal but affirming.

And thus in his most famous poem, "Love Calls Us to the Things of This World," the speaker wakes up to the apparently mundane. From his apartment bed he looks out his window to see people's laundry on the lines strung across the sky, a sight most of us would consider ugly, a sight that would inspire Lowell to write about the depressing ghosts in his brilliant and self-centered life. Wilbur's speaker, however, is enthralled by bed sheets, blouses, and smocks: "the morning air is all awash with angels." Please note that the poet takes us back down from the laundry in the air to the body in bed, from soul to body so to speak, with careful images of the rhythm of human two-sidedness, good and bad.

> The soul . . . cries,
>   "Oh, let there be nothing on earth but laundry,
> Nothing but rosy hands in the rising steam
> And clear dances done in the sight of heaven."
>
>   Yet, as the sun acknowledges
> With a warm look the world's hunks and colors,
> The soul descends once more in bitter love
> To accept the waking body, saying now
> In a changed voice as the man yawns and rises,
>   "Bring them down from their ruddy gallows;
> Let there be clean linen for the backs of thieves;
> Let lovers go fresh and sweet to be undone,
> And the heaviest nuns walk in a pure floating
> Of dark habits,
>   keeping their difficult balance."

Mark Each Day

"It's snowing still," said Eeyore gloomily.
"So it is."
"And freezing."
"Is it?"
"Yes," said Eeyore. "However," he said, brightening up a little,
"we haven't had an earthquake lately."

—A. A. Milne, *The House at Pooh Corner*

In 1906, a 7.9–8.2 earthquake hit San Francisco at 5:12 a.m. Over three thousand people died, more than the death toll of the terrorist attacks on 9/11. All the brick buildings except one crumbled and fell, and then, like a call and response from hell, fires began to shoot up from the earth and burn for days.

"San Francisco is gone," the soon-to-be-famous American author Jack London wrote. "Its industrial section is wiped out. Its business section is wiped out. Its social and residential section is wiped out. The factories and warehouses, the great stores and newspaper buildings, the hotels and the palaces of the nabobs, are all gone."

In talking to the survivors, London noticed a theme: how a shock of mere seconds, when the earth moves, changes expectations—in the way we see the world (including cathedral towers and gigantic cranes) and in the way we see our lives. Put simply, cracks open.

"I saw an old man," London wrote, "on crutches. Said he: 'Today is my birthday. Last night I was worth thirty thousand dollars. I bought five bottles of wine, some delicate fish and other things for my birthday dinner. [Today] I have had no dinner, and all I own are these crutches.'" London moved on to another house. "I went inside with the owner. He was cool and cheerful and hospitable. 'Yesterday morning,' he said, 'I was worth six hundred thousand dollars. This morning this house is all I have left. It will go in fifteen minutes.' He pointed to a large cabinet. 'That is my wife's collection of china. This rug upon which we stand is a present. It cost fifteen hundred dollars. Try that piano. Listen to its tone. There are few like it. There are no horses. The flames will be here in fifteen minutes.'"

I could go on, with example after example from London's descriptions of the 1906 earthquake to other earthquakes and hurricanes, to the times in our lives, when our expectations of another normal day, in a lifetime of days under *our* control, headed toward *our* goals, expectations, and dreams, come crashing down with the force and terror of broken statues falling off our cathedral towers and a crane, brought in to repair the towers, collapsing on South Road. I quickly say no one was killed here, shockingly. My purpose is not to compare the earthquake that surprised Washington, D.C., in 2011, to quakes that kill thousands but simply to accentuate the essential fact of the surprise.

Looking back at our ancestors and what they might have assumed about their lives and their futures, and what control they might have assumed they possessed over their lives and futures, should remind us that, if we see life as a game of ownership and control, we lose; if we believe we can predict and control the future, we are fools.

Oh yes, the future will always be there, until it is not.

There is no greater wisdom than the cliché you hear time and again, that living life a day at a time is enough. Who, obsessed by the future, would have imagined an earthquake not on the west coast but on the east, a crane falling without hitting a single person, safety fences and walkways constructed, parking and traffic nearly impossible. And yet X, Y, and Z might still happen this year, and I am too superstitious to name what events or steps or procedures X, Y, and Z might represent. But we can't be certain. We can never be certain.

Author Flannery O'Connor, whom I deeply respect, so believed in the prospect and challenge of living one day, even surviving it, that she spoke not of something sweet—like "stop and smell the roses"—but of that which is "terrifying." I like that: the terror of one day at a time. The terror of earthquakes and hurricanes and accidents is real enough, but have you ever imagined how challenging and even frightening life might be if you tried to live one day as fully as you can, without thinking about tomorrow. If we did, I believe we would not live in the fear that something bad would happen—my goodness, we only have twenty-four hours—but we would live so we would not miss the astonishing and good things, the power and glory that live in the here and now, the smell and shape of mud and flower and tree, the grip of friends, the gift of learning, the joy of one breath deep in the lungs. How life, if you pay attention, can overflow.

These are romantic words. Here are specific suggestions. Make yourself mark each day. You can do this by establishing what medieval monks call a rule: Every day at set-aside times, force yourself to stop. Force yourself to do the same thing at that same time each day. Make it relate to being alive and being conscious of it. Say a prayer, read a reflection, keep still, and know what a gift it is to breathe. Or keep a history. Every day write about the day: what happened, how it felt, what it means this moment for you to be alive. Or create something. Sing a song or write one. Sketch a tree. These simple acts, if done with discipline, help us prepare for the moments when the soul opens up to something beyond us and teaches us to say, from deep in the heart and soul, thanks be to God.

• *18* •

The Road to Emmaus

A Language of God

But Peter got up and ran to the tomb; stooping and looking in, he saw the linen cloths by themselves; then he went home, amazed at what had happened.

—Luke 24:12 (NRSV)

*O*n the same day that Peter rushes to the tomb to find it empty, two disciples are walking away from Jerusalem toward the town of Emmaus, seven miles distant. Luke says, "They were talking with each other about all these things that had happened"—the Last Supper, Peter's betrayal of Jesus, the trial and torture, Jesus' silence, and the Crucifixion. Jesus' three years of ministry, which these two disciples hoped would lead to kingship and the end of the Roman burden, were lost. He had died on a cross beside common criminals. His disciples suffered nothing less than abject despair.

Instead of keeping the stranger who joins them on the road mysterious to us, Luke tells us that Jesus himself "came near and went with them, but their eyes were kept from recognizing him." We delight in the dramatic irony that we're in the know and the players on stage know less than we do. They had spent three years with him. We ask ourselves, what is wrong with these guys? Why can't they see?

Not recognizing is the leitmotif of the resurrection stories. Mary weeps at the empty tomb and asks the gardener where they have taken his body. Then "she turned around and saw Jesus standing there but she did not know it was Jesus." Some disciples return to their previous occupation, fishing: "Just after daybreak, Jesus stood on the beach; but the disciples did not know that it was Jesus."

There is a distinction between perception and recognition. Perception is "the act of being aware or conscious of a thing through our five senses." It can

56

sometimes be unreliable. As a child I visited haunted houses. In a darkened room, someone took my hand and stuck it onto a plate full of spaghetti and in ghostly voice said I was feeling a raw brain. Touch said this was true—it sure felt the way I imagined a brain did. I did not realize the falsity of this by my five senses alone. I had to think. I had to understand that they were deceiving my touch. There are innumerable examples of realities we know about beyond the proof of one or all of our senses. The disciples see a man on the shore but think it is someone they don't know.

This fact does not in any way prove the idea of resurrection, but it is another example in the truth that reality transcends any model we can create for it. But it might be worth imagining resurrection differently, even if it's not going to help us prove it factually, as nothing will until we die. To be clear, I am not saying that resurrection isn't something beyond death but that one truth about it might, as they say without irony, be right in front of our eyes. Filmmaker Errol Morris calls this the difference between "seeing is believing" and "believing is seeing."

When the stranger walking with the two disciples asks them why they are so sad, the one named Cleopas says, "Are you the only stranger in Jerusalem who does not know the things that have taken place there in these days?" I hear great anger in this response. I imagine Cleopas wants to grab the stranger by the throat and say, "Listen, the man whom I gave my all to, whom I sacrificed my all for, whom I loved, is dead. He was tortured and killed, and you ask me why I am so sad?" Luke writes that Cleopas goes on to say, "We had hoped that he was the one to redeem Israel."

Then the miracle happens. He lectures them on Scripture and Christ's fulfillment of it; they find themselves so moved by his words that they urge him to stay. They take bread together, bless it and break it, as they had done four days earlier, though the two men have yet to recognize the connection. Then, in one of the finest lines in Scripture, "their eyes were opened, and they recognized him."

Their belief finally allowed them to see a different reality.

Nearly two thousand years later, in the summer of 1939 in North Carolina, a six-year-old boy walked from his parents' house through a large pine wood to his grandmother's house. In the middle of the woods he experienced the presence of God. For the first time then, and in "unpredictable and widely spaced intervals" until 1983, this boy felt what he called "demonstrations." They never lasted more than a few seconds but seemed, in retrospect, hours long—a time warp for impossible-to-explain spiritual reasons. This boy was not crazy then. He was not crazy for the rest of his life. The demonstrations felt like "breakings-in" upon his consciousness. This is what he wrote: "All of visible and invisible nature ([him]self included) [was] a single reality, a single thought from a central mind."

I'm not a mystic, and I think anyone who feels he has intimations of God's will must check those suspicions with reason, Scripture, experience, and the church. But I am human, and I believe that the deepest part of all our humanity allows us to have glimpses of God, to hear syllables, even unearthly musical phrases, especially if we're willing to assume that our seeing regardless of belief is not enough.

Two disciples on the road to Emmaus, after "something kept them from seeing," have their eyes opened to the presence of their risen Lord as he breaks bread with them. Then we hear from Reynolds Price as a six-year-old boy. He went on to write thirty-three books of essays, poetry collections, and novels, and was a member of the American Academy of Arts and Letters. I cite his testament because I don't want you to think that prestigious people today discount a language of God as being the work of only the ancients.

Most mystics from every religious tradition agree that we cannot will God's presence in our lives. But I strongly believe an effort of will prepares us for God, even if, to use Reynolds Price's word, the demonstration comes totally unawares. The disciples were kept from seeing by their own anxieties. Aren't we all? Only when they listened with their hearts to a complete stranger and then broke bread did they see. Reynolds Price was visited for the first time in the depths of a natural silence, without any preparation other than to be six years old.

Asked for spiritual directions, I might suggest finding time to keep silence. Pray. Try to feel God's presence when you do—that is enough. Study. Read the Scriptures, read literature, study the natural world, read everything as a dialogue not only between you and the author, but between you, the author, and God.

Directions and recipes are never enough. The Bible is full of stories of angels taking on human guise and talking to other humans—Abraham, Jacob, and Daniel are three examples from the Hebrew Bible. The story of the road to Emmaus shows two disciples assuming the risen Lord is a human stranger. I think the words other people say to you—whether they are friends or total strangers—are sometimes angelic. I mean they can on occasion be words intended for you from God. They are spiritual messages, and they are not always comforting. Sometimes they are harsh. Just listen.

God can be very strange indeed.

· 19 ·

Faith, Vocation, and Work

*W*hen I was twenty-four, I copied this passage from Georges Bernanos's *Diary of a Country Priest* (1954): "Faith is not a thing one 'loses,' we merely cease to shape our lives by it." If we are in the "faith" game, we must believe it exists as an active force to shape our lives and the lives we work with daily. But let me be honest. I would prefer not. It scares me. At times it promises certainty, but doesn't it also promise risk, loss of control, pain, and doubt about the materialistic world? I prefer to speak of it in hallowed and safely put-away terms.

After I graduated from college, the Vietnam War was ending, and my medical deferment freed me and shackled me with guilt. Suddenly, though, I could travel. The externals of life were normal: I was one of those who went abroad to study. The internals were a mess (which is normal but unacknowledged by a twenty-four-year-old). Lost in the romantic myth, I imagined that I escaped the shackles of a Southern Baptist upbringing, four confusing years at college (three of the four years the students were on strike), and a possible marriage to a brilliant and beautiful medical student (which both of us realized later would be another mistake in our error-prone lives). And yet I was my hero, James Joyce (I got in line with thousands of others), because he left Dublin, never returned, and in "silence, exile, and cunning" became great. I would also write, but with biblical power about my troubled homeland and screwed-up family. I would forge in the smithy of my soul the conscience of America.

There is nothing, absolutely nothing, like our youthful dreams, is there? I was soaked by the jazz of fantasy and self-delusion but also hope and ambition and brassy energy. And like so many of my present-day students, I did more envisioning than working. I saw myself called to be a writer more than

59

I actually wrote. I was a Noun—a person of distinction—and not a Verb—to act on my dream. Let us remember the cart of riches is pulled by a plough horse.

Then we grow up and learn how to pull that plough.

My confusion was authentic in that nothing about it wasn't genuinely felt. Now that I live in the last third of my life and have position, I feel the loss of that genuineness. Perhaps those called to the priesthood know what I mean about being a Something now. Have you at one time or another suffered the discovery that your very position to which you were called can actually obstruct your life of faith? On some days are you more tied to the collar (and "by" it) than to the One whom the collar signifies? All too often I become more enamored of the glorious position of Headmaster than I am to mastering anything, a Gilbert and Sullivan admiral who stuck to his desk and never went to sea and "polished up the handle so carefullee / that now [he's] the ruler of the Queen's Navee."

What endears me to the stories in the Bible is the fitfulness of the narrative. We beg for our stories to be linear (and, you could argue, deceitful in being so), but fitfulness feels more life-like. I feel this way, but I grow up, but then I realize I haven't grown up, and then I pull the plough and find a position held in high regard, and then I question my own genuineness, and then I give a speech and all is revealed, until later that night, at least, when I wonder what in God's name was I saying.

In his marvelous collection of homilies, *With Love and Prayers,* Tony Jarvis, longtime headmaster of the Roxbury Latin School, cites James Thurber's "The Sea and the Shore."

The story is about lemmings. The rodents, most centrally located in Norway, periodically make unexpected mass migrations from the land into the sea and certain death. Thurber attempts to explain with his typical humor. One lemming leads the way toward the sea having shouted, "Fire! The world is coming to an end!" The other lemmings panic and follow him, lemming-like, rushing headlong to their death. As they die, however, some shout, "We are saved!" Others shout, "We are lost!" Thurber's moral graces the story: "All men should strive to learn before they die what they are running from, and to, and why."

I laugh, but ever since being doused in the Dostoyevsky fire, I can see no other way but leaping (so does Tony Jarvis). Yes, you need to study, pray, and live so that you choose a path that is your own (which can't help, frankly, to be at least a little lemming-like), and then you leap without full certainty. Thurber's parable is about thoughtlessness and social pressure. My response is, well, you can't avoid the cliff or the uncertainty.

"He that undertakes to believe," John Bunyan writes, "sets upon the hardest task that ever was proposed to man. . . . Believing is sweating work. . . .

Run for heaven, fight for heaven, labour for heaven, wrestle for heaven, or you will like go without it." I once spent a good deal of time with a man who as a youth corresponded with Flannery O'Connor. "Faith is a gift," she wrote him, "but the will has a great deal to do with it. The loss of it is basically a failure of appetite, assisted by a sterile intellect. Some people when they lose their faith in Christ substitute a swollen faith in themselves. . . . Let me tell you this: Faith comes and goes. It rises and falls like the tides of an invisible ocean. If it is presumptuous to think that faith will stay with you forever, it is just as presumptuous to think that unbelief will . . . if you find in yourself the least return of a desire for faith . . . go back to the church with a light heart and without the conscience-raking to which you are probably subject. Subtlety is the curse of man. It is not found in the deity" (*The Habit of Being: Letters of Flannery O'Connor*).

Perhaps I'm cursed at trying to be too subtle. Take comfort in Flannery O'Connor's admonition that belief comes and goes, and that we work in our daily callings, that we must assert our will for faith, and that, without regard to human subtlety, God is always there, alpha and omega.

IV

LOOKING OUTWARD

Service

· 20 ·

For God and for the State

$\mathcal{A}$ boy named Dietrich was born in 1906 in southeastern Germany. A prominent German psychiatrist in Berlin, his father recognized his son was a superior student and educated him well. At the age of twenty-one, the precocious Dietrich received a doctorate in theology from the University of Berlin but was too young to be ordained. He came to the United States for more study but returned to Berlin in 1931, where he helped to found a new Protestant church, the Confessing Church.

A boy named James Harvey was born in 1911, five years after Dietrich, in Pittsburgh. A prominent church organist in the Episcopal Church, his father also recognized his son was a superior student and educated him well. He sent James Harvey to a relatively new boys' school, St. Albans School in Washington. Precocious James Harvey graduated as a junior from St. Albans and attended Harvard, where he majored in languages and by his twenties was fluent in seven.

In 1939 World War II began. In his pulpit Dietrich Bonhoeffer had spoken so passionately against Hitler and his anti-Semitic policies that the Gestapo banned him from preaching. He then became associated with high-ranking military officers and their "July Plot" to assassinate Hitler. They failed. When the Nazis discovered that Bonhoeffer's money had been used to assist Jews fleeing to Switzerland, he was arrested in April 1943 and imprisoned, first in Berlin and ultimately in the Flossenbürg concentration camp.

Because of his facility in languages, when the war began, James Harvey Gaul, St. Albans class of 1928, enlisted in the Office of Strategic Services (the OSS). In 1944, serving in England, he became deputy head of the Dawes Mission. That fall, Gaul, a British officer who headed the mission, and their twelve men parachuted behind German lines into Slovakia. All official communication was cut off. They were ordered to escape detection, find British and American pilots who had been downed on bombing raids and were rumored to be hiding there, and work with underground resistance movements to transport the pilots out of Slovakia either to Russia or to the Mediterranean and back to safety. None of the men on the mission were heard from for the rest of the war.

On April 9, 1945, three weeks before the liberation of Berlin, Dietrich Bonhoeffer—pastor, writer, theologian, German patriot—was executed as a traitor.

No one had word of James Harvey Gaul. After the war, a classmate dedicated himself to finding out what happened. He learned that after a few months in hiding, the members of the Dawes Mission were discovered on December 25, 1944, in an isolated cabin in the Slovakian forest by German troops tipped off by local residents. (The night before, James Harvey Gaul had conducted a Christmas Eve service for his fellow soldiers.) They were surrounded and forced to surrender. Sometime in January 1944, James Harvey Gaul—co-leader of the group, OSS officer, St. Albans alumnus, and American patriot—was executed as a spy.

These two men, burning with faith and courage, were willing to die for their beliefs. In the 1930s Dietrich wanted to go to India to study nonviolence with Mahatma Gandhi, but the German government would not let him travel. Even with his interest in nonviolence, he supported the assassination attempt against Hitler. The pastor himself did not take up arms and in fact was remembered fondly by his prison guards because he supported both the guards and his fellow prisoners during the Allied air raids on Berlin. He led all of them in singing hymns while the bombs destroyed the city around him. I suspect he forgave his executioners as they strung him up on a meat hook from the ceiling and tied a piano wire around his neck.

In a dark night James Harvey showed courage enough to parachute far behind German lines. What chance of survival did he believe he had? James Harvey was described by those who knew him as a man of faith, someone who thought what he was doing—fighting in a war—was right and what God wanted him to do.

I think about these parallel stories as I meditate on the St. Albans School hymn, written with Victorian prose at the beginning of the twentieth century by the headmaster's wife, Edith Church, written for a school uniquely positioned to include students whose parents have a lot to do with the running of the state, written at a time when the Episcopal Church was nearly the established church in, if not power, then influence: Each verse ends with the rolling phrase we lustily sing, "For God and for the State."

Show forth a spirit gen'rous, true
For God and for the State.

The call is now to every man
For God and for the State.

To fight the wrong and show the good
In serving God and State.

For him who triumphs with his life
For God and for the State.

We love the hymn but know its complications. The conjunction "and" in these verses can be deeply problematic, for God and the state do not always walk hand in hand. Bonhoeffer's God told him to fight not with but against the German state. Gaul's God told him to fight for God and the American state. In the safety of seventy-five years' distance, we believe these decisions were fitting.

But what if Bonhoeffer had decided to be a soldier for the German state? What if with other commandoes he came ashore from a submarine onto Long Island (a true episode, but of course without Bonhoeffer) and was captured and executed, like Gaul, as a spy? The order to execute the Germans without trial came from the president of the United States. And what if Gaul, a deeply religious man, decided that the United States should not go to war against Germany (as American hero Charles Lindbergh believed). What if he had been sent to jail the way Bonhoeffer was, the way the American poet and conscientious objector Robert Lowell was?

Nearly all of us feel World War II was a just war. But please remember how many "good Germans" chose to serve their state because they automatically linked God and state. And of course the majority of our country did not want to stop Hitler until after we were attacked at Pearl Harbor. Isolationists were known to say that God surrounded us with oceans for a reason. We must consider. The past can never be a clear and single narrative. To prove the point, all I need do is mention a few issues involving God and the state in the present. Feel the emotion roll through you as you read this simple list: waterboarding, Iraq, weapons of mass destruction, September 11, Afghanistan, Abu Ghraib, female suicide bombers, Guantanamo Bay, the presidential election.

I believe as humans and citizens we must actively engage. I proclaim the Ten Commandments. I proclaim the two great commandments of the New Testament: Love the Lord your God with all your heart, all your mind, and all your soul. Do unto others as you would have them do unto you. I also love this state, the United States of America, especially when it argues that all of us are created equal in the sight of the law and thus have equal rights and responsibilities, which we will defend when actually threatened. One of the many reasons I love this school is that we sing together. Very few schools in this country, with the exception of military preps, speak of God and state as often as we do. But when we next sing our school hymn, let us remember all its admonitions that lead up to its magnificent declaration:

> . . . make your lives what God has planned
> . . . suppress all fear and hate
> . . . fight the wrong and show the good
> . . . love casts [all fear] away
> For God and for the State.

I Will Sing Unto the Lord

I keep a flag atop the bookshelf in my office, as an act of honor. To understand the story of this particular flag, however, I need to give some brief context. My grandmother's hero was William Jennings Bryan, four-time candidate for president of the United States, defender of the silver standard, secretary of state for Woodrow Wilson, a teetotaler, and the prosecutor in the Scopes trial. He argued in favor of a fundamentalist interpretation of the creation story versus Clarence Darrow's defense of Mr. Scopes and the theory of evolution. My grandmother's hero worship was so severe that, like many of her contemporaries, she named her son after William Jennings Bryan. And here the story of this flag begins.

Every story worth listening to must be built around a problem. As a boy, I didn't get it. I didn't understand what the problem was. All I knew was that my mother's younger brother, Wilson Jennings Mehaffey, was a good uncle. He was called Turk because in the mountains of North Carolina his red hair was described as a "turkey" red color. The nickname was shortened, and it stuck. He was a blast to be with as a boy. He told jokes and had an infectious laugh. He slipped me candy whenever my mother wasn't looking. He loved football and followed my school teams closely and, on Sunday afternoons when he was in town, would watch the games with my father and me. Most important, though, he was a great storyteller. My parents thought children should be sheltered from problematic stories about their families. Uncle Turk didn't think so. He would tell me the stories Mom and Dad wouldn't.

Uncle Turk told me about a hunting accident in which one of my grandfather's brothers was accidentally killed. He told me about the time my grandfather, a lifelong railroad conductor, leapt off the back of his train onto a runaway car and stopped it from barreling down a mountainside. The

Asheville *Citizen-Times* called my grandfather a hero. Uncle Turk told me about Granddaddy's ongoing game with the train engineer. They would stop a train near picnic tables so he and the engineer could get out and have standing broad jump contests from the ground to the top of the tables. Of course none of the passengers knew what was going on. He explained to me that in the late 1920s and early 1930s, my mother could not go on a date without another adult female chaperone walking twenty feet behind her. He laughed about how their parents would scare them at Halloween, sneaking outside in the middle of the night to scratch the screens on the windows with their fingernails. And he would narrate the great revivals that would climax with the baptisms in the streams of the North Carolina mountains, laughing that people turned blue not from the Holy Spirit but from the frigid water, and implying as he spoke a great heresy, that too many people were fascinated with the religion of his namesake, William Jennings Bryan. Whenever I asked my mother and father follow-up questions, I was told that children were to be seen and not heard.

But there was a problem with Uncle Turk. How did I know? I would come into rooms and hear his name, and my parents would see me and stop talking. I would overhear arguments from behind closed doors. Mother would keep referring to two women—Dorothy and Suzanne—and I think I was fourteen before I realized that the first was my uncle's former wife and the second his daughter. I had never met them because in a family that admired Mr. Bryan's way of thinking, divorce was a sin. I would hear my dad say that Turk had already lost two jobs and there was no chance anyone would ever hire him again. My mother's name was Jerry. I can remember hearing Dad say, "It's hopeless, Jerry. I tell you, it's hopeless."

My grandfather the railroad conductor died on Christmas Day in 1967. This was particular difficult for my mother and father because Christmas Day was the anniversary of their wedding, so for the rest of their lives they remembered both their marriage and my grandfather's death on the same day. We buried Granddaddy and had the family home in Asheville open to everyone afterwards. The next day the extended family, without grandmother the widow, went out to eat together before going to our separate homes. In the middle of the dinner, my mother's youngest sister's husband and my favorite uncle Turk began ragging on each other. Before I knew what happened, they stood up and said they were going outside into the parking lot to beat the pulp out of each other. One man said to the other he was a coward, and the other responded, "You're just a good-for-nothing drunk." My older brother was at the Naval Academy then, and he dragged me with him outside to stand with my father between the two pugilists and stop them. I was trying to hold my arms out against my favorite uncle, but I had trouble recognizing him with such rage in his face.

When my father had calmed the two men down and made my brother and me go back inside, I saw my mother in tears. She looked up at me and cited a verse from the Book of Psalms: "How long must we have sorrow in our hearts?"

As I said, every story has a problem. Stories also have to flash back into the past to explain the problem. Let's do that with my uncle. Apparently he was an astonishing teenager. His name takes on more irony, I believe, because in many ways he was a young turk, or what we later might have called a stud. He was the first man in my entire family, either side, to go to college. He was considered one of the great football players in western North Carolina, so General Neyland at the University of Tennessee (the football stadium in Knoxville is named after this coach) invited him to play football for the Volunteers. There, he became closest friends with another player, and together when they graduated they joined the Navy. When I was old enough to start investigating the problem in the family, I found some photographs in my grandmother's cabinet. The first was the wedding portrait of my uncle and his extraordinarily beautiful bride—the Dorothy I had never met. Next to the bride and bridegroom was his closest friend (both men dressed in their Navy uniforms). Another portrait I found was of my mother's entire family in the home in Asheville. I realized that this portrait was intentionally made to capture them together, perhaps for the last time, before my uncle was shipped overseas at the start of World War II.

At the very beginning of our entry into the war, the Germans pummeled the American ships and the troops who went into the Mediterranean and North Africa. It took us a while to get our war machine going effectively, and even so, when they talk now of a unit in Iraq with a serious number of fatalities, military people use the phrase "a World War II rate of casualties"—in other words, tough. I will cut to the chase here. My uncle's best friend served with him on the same ship. In a particularly brutal battle in the first few months of the war—I cannot bother you with the details, because I don't know them—my uncle's friend was killed. He died in my uncle's arms. Forty-five years later, I stood beside my uncle in a hospital bed (I was trying to get him dried out from an alcoholic haze), and he sat up in the bed, tears in his eyes, and said to me, referring to his best friend's death, "I just couldn't keep his guts inside of him."

Now let's fast forward to the end. The problem that I didn't understand, of course, was what happened when my uncle came home from the war. He tried to live as a normal GI. His daughter Suzanne was born. But in only a few years, Dorothy took Suzanne with her to Richmond and divorced him. His family, a family that held fast to a literal interpretation of the Bible, loved him dearly, but we could not cope with his alcoholism and blamed the bottle and not the war. Our faces were full of judgment. He could not keep any job longer than a year. After my parents moved us to Tampa, Florida, my uncle would come down to visit but go missing. My father would force me to come with him to find Uncle Turk. We would check out the bars where my uncle became known for hanging out, and we would sometimes find him before noon at a bar with a beer and a shot of whiskey in front of him. Then my grandfather died and the fight ensued the day after his funeral, and I clearly understood what the problem was.

Alcohol deceives you about who you truly are. Its marketers promise joy, but it finds a weakness in you and exploits it. There can be a genetic disposition toward alcoholism, but it is never that simple nor is it, in the end, a legitimate excuse. Alcoholism is usually not a problem in isolation, but a symptom of our problems—to phrase it much too simply, our inability to turn our desires, for a diagnostic manual full of reasons, away from the sorrows my mother sang of to the bounty of this life. Perhaps that sounds trite or too religious for your taste. But if I had the power to give a gift from God, I would pray that we learned to live more simply and more fully into life and sing about it.

I eventually left Tampa to go on with my life, going to college and graduate school, beginning work, getting married, until my wife and I returned to Asheville to teach at a boarding school. My children were born, so my life was taken up with my own young family. After my grandmother died, my uncle returned to the family home in Bryson City, a small town at the edge of the Great Smoky Mountain Park, and over the next six years I would get calls from his friends and his doctors asking me to drive the hour and a half from Asheville and take him out of the hospital, where they would send him to dry out after another night of binge drinking. They asked me to stop him from drinking, and of course I could not. One night he died alone in a boarding house.

His wife Dorothy did not come to the funeral—she was close to death herself—but his daughter Suzanne came, and after one refusal after another, I finally accepted from her the flag that the Navy honored my uncle with, for indeed his service during World War II had been heroic. "He would want you to have it," she said.

His life turned terrible and miserable because of his drinking and because of the deeper problems, most of them from the war, his drinking disguised. Perhaps he had post-traumatic stress syndrome and thought drinking made it better; all of us can deceive ourselves into thinking alcohol fixes our problem. As terrible as his life became, though, he remains immensely significant to me. I call him a hero, a troubled hero, but I also tell his story just to emphasize how the battleground and subsequent drinking brought down a young turk like my uncle, a hero who did not have access to the kind of mental care he needed after the war.

But my uncle answered the call. He suffered greatly. I wish he could have been able to come through, for many men who suffered as much did come through. But who cannot forgive him? And finally, in the middle of his sorrowful life, he still cared for me and told me great stories. Today I sing his story.

· 22 ·

The Philosopher's Stone

I often remind my English students not to sell a word short. When this school's third headmaster, Albert Lucas, asked his boys in the 1930s and 1940s what the word "service" implied, might they have thought of "military" service and then figured they had the measure of the word? Some of our fourth headmaster's young scholars, because Charles Martin was an influential priest, might have decided upon "divine" service. Many young people today, I believe, would speak only of "community" service or "social" service. If any of us pigeonhole the concept of service, however, we do it an injustice. While at first blush a call to multiply the ways young people think of service might not seem that important, in this particular case a pigeonholed definition works against our ultimate goals for children.

Educators of my generation have tried to teach students with advantages of material goods and good health to share their goods with people who do not have the same advantages—the poor, the hungry, the blind, the infirm. The children of Israel were to let the produce of the land lie fallow every seventh year so that the poor shall eat. Christ says, "For when I was hungry, you gave me food." We have tried to encourage social-mindedness by creating a required social service program and even making graduation contingent upon the requisite number of community service hours. The state of Maryland, in fact, legislates service hours for the young.

The paradoxes of a required social service program are glaring. We necessitate an action that by its very nature should be voluntary. In doing so we imply that it is not naturally voluntary. We also measure it by hours as if it were work for pay. And sometimes we teach a lesson we don't intend. We might profess doing good service, for example, or being moral in our service, but unintentionally we signal to the students that the human interchange is

74

only one way. We serve; they receive. We hand over the literal goods, but since the other person doesn't have the same quantity of goods, that person can offer us nothing (except, perhaps, allowing him- or herself to be a projection for our sense of our own goodness). Thus the concept of charity, which in Middle English included in it the idea of fairness and equity—and still should—becomes complicated in the student's mind with a handout, or more accurately, a hand down.

These paradoxes will not disappear. Whatever the political theories, true equity will never be a reality, nor will we ever lose the virtue of charity. Business gurus speak of "managing up" and "managing down." We must teach that a broad understanding of service—down, level, or up, to be crude—enriches the narrower idea the phrase "community service" unfortunately has become.

The terrible events of the fall of 2001, for example, remind us that service should transcend the materialistic fault lines of our culture. The young people we teach witnessed and felt extreme suffering and fear in all manner of people: They saw handouts that were literally that—any number of people, rich and poor, extending a hand to someone else, rich or poor, pulling the person up or out or into some kind of safety. Suddenly for our young, the word "service" exploded. It suddenly meant firefighters and police and emergency workers more than it did social workers and soup kitchen volunteers. Firefighters, then, were no longer irritants who made us do fire drills but heroes. Police were not people to be scorned for ticketing us but heroes. Soldiers were once again heroes. Let us help our young people sustain this pride in our public servants. At the same time, let us teach them that a society is healthiest when many rather than a few are celebrated as servants and, in fact, that all vocations in society, even those in the tall buildings of lower Manhattan where the temptation for greed is hard to resist, still offer the opportunity to serve.

We are to seek out the poor and hungry in particular—we must not forget that. Christ would not have said, "You gave *me* food . . . you gave *me* drink . . . you took *me* into your home . . . you clothed *me*," if he did not intend to incarnate the poor, the hungry, the blind, and the infirm with his own spiritual dignity and power. In response, St. Albans will always teach its students to serve the disadvantaged. But that can never be enough.

Our daily mode should be one of service, *to whomever we come across, wherever we are*. Think of the angel Raphael's explanation to Adam in *Paradise Lost*: "Freely we serve / Because we freely love." We serve each other at school and at home every day because we are free to do so, and we should choose to serve communities outside ourselves—other schools, this city, this nation, this world. If we do not have a sense that our daily mode of living isn't rooted in service, then we will slip into that very frustration I began this essay with. We devalue the poor if we think only in terms of service as a hand down.

The fall of 2001 reminded us that society, in the best sense of the word, is essential to our individual survival, that we will never escape the threats against life, nor find meaning in life, if we run away and hide, whether in the tundra or right here, behind the economic fault lines of gated communities or world trade centers or investments. We must be all in this, together. Think of service as *public* service—an advocating for justice, peace, and goodness *for all*. We will continue to read to the blind or serve soup or tithe, but that's not enough, in the same way that fulfilling a graduation requirement for social service isn't enough. Service is all in all, meaning and necessity, whether in business or law or medicine or public service. We require it, but we require more: the creation of service as a habit.

In talking with my students about the habit of service, I find the metaphor of concentric circles effective. They can respond to the picture of a stone tossed into the middle of a lake, or a target at the end of an archery range, or even the heart as the core of a human being. At the center, which I refer to not as the bull's-eye dead center but as the center of life, you must hold a belief that meaning in your life comes from serving that which is good beyond the self. That sentence may imply all sorts of complicated things having to do with an individual, but I tend to think it simply means that your belief is not simply that God or a God exists, but that purpose to your life comes when you determine to serve in this life the goodness that God stands for.

"Elixir," like "service," is a prince of a word. It is the alchemical preparation that turns metals into gold, what has historically been known as the philosopher's stone.

Another definition is the quintessence or kernel of a thing. George Herbert's 1633 poem "The Elixir" has for me always captured what service most essentially is (the poem is also hymn 592 in the 1982 Hymnal). I will not cite the entire piece, only its beginning and end. The first stanza reads,

> Teach me, my God and King
> In all things Thee to see,
> And what I do in any thing
> To do it as for Thee.

The subsequent four stanzas ask God for the ability to reflect upon all our action and make it solely service, with the knowledge that working, even at drudgery, for God's sake, is the famous stone

> That turneth all to gold.
> For that which God doth touch and own
> Cannot for less be told.

Good Time, Inhuman Time

$\mathcal{M}$y grandmother kept scrapbooks. Dutifully, she scissored out gossip from newspapers, kept postcards from Florida or letters home from the wives of my father and his brothers, and collected a thousand and one other odd fragments of family life, pasting them into creaky books with paper browned with age. My grandmother's contemporary, Albert Lucas, the third headmaster of St. Albans School (1929–1949), shared her passion. My favorites, throughout all the pages of the five scrapbooks Canon Lucas compiled, are those incisive, sometimes ironic, commentaries he wrote, in a meticulous hand, next to the "scraps" he collected.

Take a 1944 photograph, for example. Angus Dun is consecrated as the fourth bishop of Washington. The camera peers down on the crossing of the far-from-completed cathedral, where in keeping with the ancient practice of the Church, all the bishops in attendance circle the kneeling Dun and lay their hands on his head. On the photograph, Canon Lucas wrote the name of each bishop down the length of his billowy sleeve. In the article accompanying the photograph, this paragraph is underlined: "The brightest hood in the cathedral was worn by Canon Albert Lucas, who served as the presiding Bishop's chaplain. It blended nicely with his red hair." Next to the paragraph the Chief wrote, "Not much of a commendation."

While the consecration of Bishop Dun was clearly a high and holy event for our community, surely some people that April day in 1944 felt a disquiet similar to the way many of us have felt recently. Our days on earth, here in Washington, D.C., with our country at war in Iraq, are surely different from the circumstances of 1944. Nevertheless, we know the disquiet between the "here" and the "there"—"here" the obligation to provide safety and routine for the sake of our children growing up, while "there" soldiers and civilians alike have suffered and died in unconscionable ways. On the day Bishop Dun was consecrated, for example, five B-17 bombers—with none of their crew surviving—were shot down over Kassel, Germany, after inflicting heavy damage on an airfield. The Soviets bombed Sevastopol while Hitler's Operation Order No. 7 ordered the German army to recapture the Crimea. Planes from the USS *Saratoga* battled Japanese planes in the Indian Ocean, and the Nazis were following up their invasion of Hungary by moving 430,000 Hungarian Jews to Auschwitz-Birkenau. The critic George Steiner refers to this juxtaposition of events within the same time as "the time relation" and speculates whether the ancient Gnostics were right in thinking that there were different species of time in the same world—"good time" and "inhuman time," in which "men fall into the slow hands of living damnation."

Few school heads knew better than World War I Marine Albert Lucas what "inhuman time" could feel like. I remain fascinated, however, by how hard he tried, during inhuman times, to provide good and normal lives for the very boys who would eventually serve in the armed forces and die for their country. Canon Lucas writes a letter from the headmaster's study that encourages fathers to sit with their sons prior to their going to bed at night so that they can share time together and talk. He doesn't write, ". . . to talk about the war." In his scrapbook, he pastes photographs from the *News-Ledger* under the title "Happy Days." The photographs picture the undefeated St. Albans football team with Albert Lucas Jr.'s picture. Turn the page to picture the undefeated 1942 team. He cuts out a photograph of a large crane in front of the school's Lane-Johnston Building, where the roof is being replaced (some things never change). Then he puts exclamation marks next to the newspaper article that says Jimmie Trimble (from the St. Albans class of 1943) has signed a professional baseball contract with the Washington Senators. He even includes an article about a priest resigning at St. Stephen's-Incarnation and the furor over that. No war news to be found. I can almost hear him saying to himself, "The boys will grow up soon enough, soon enough."

It cannot last. Time in the scrapbooks shifts from good to inhuman. Nearly all the scraps in the last pages of the longest volume are devoted to St. Albans boys in the war, in particular Albert Jr., a marine on the USS *Nevada* during the Normandy invasion and in the Pacific. In a letter home, Canon Lucas announces that alumnus Damon Cummings (class of 1927) has been killed and Calvert Bowie (class of 1936) is missing in action. He pastes into the book a page full of the school's ration book, and then on the very last page, he includes his letter from the headmaster's study of September 19, 1945—sixteen months after the consecration of Bishop Dun. The plaque made from that letter hangs in the Lane-Johnston Building's Common Room, near the portrait of Canon Lucas. Across the top it reads *Pro Ecclesia et Pro Patria*, and it pictures many but not all of the fallen graduates of our school, including the man we felt was destined to play professional baseball, Jimmie Trimble '43.

When I was a boy and first entered an Episcopal school in 1962, the chaplain often spoke to us about "The Daily Office." By "office," the Book of Common Prayer means a rite performed as a duty, an obligation, and a service to others. We are to follow this rite "daily," making it a part of our "rule," in the sense of how we measure the hours of our life. The rule insists on the call to confess our sins even when we feel we have been virtuous and on the call to sing songs of thanksgiving even when we are close to despair. As a boy I didn't appreciate the priest's emphasis on every day, no matter what. He could have said, every day, whether here or there, whether the time is good or inhuman. Many years later, having lived through a preponderance of good time but also some suffering and the untimely death of people I love, I better understand the paradox of simultaneity.

All we can do is live our lives fully, in present circumstance, in present time. Let us worship in some way every day. Let us pray for the safety of our St. Albans boys in Kuwait and Iraq and in other places here and abroad. Let us pray for the people of Iraq and all innocents throughout the world who suffer from war. As a country let us preserve the right to free speech and yet find the courage to act for what we believe is right. Let us never believe, however, that even the most severe spiritual rule full of devout prayers, or the most overpowering army in the world, gives us control over the events of life.

One additional example from our school archives will remind us of this final point. Shelved next to Canon Lucas's scrapbooks is a large envelope sent to former archivist Elenora Brown by a person who signed his or her name simply as *N.* Canon Lucas made certain all the school's publications were forwarded to the boys at war, and he also wrote many personal letters to our graduates of the time, tracking the progress of the war, in fact, by following the lives of the St. Albans servicemen.

Across the envelope in the archives, however, *N* wrote the following note: "I can't bring myself to throw this envelope away. I suppose they should be put in the file that contains Mr. Lucas's letters to these boys, all of whom were lost in World War II." The envelope is full of unopened letters, never delivered because the men died, each envelope with a series of crossed-out addresses, the final marked "Return to the Sender," to Canon Albert Lucas at St. Albans School.

V

INSPIRING VALUES

Chancing the Arm

*I*magine we stand together in St. Patrick's Cathedral in Dublin, Ireland.

Below our feet is buried the author, satirist, and dean of St. Patrick's from 1713 to 1745, Jonathan Swift. His grave's epitaph is famous: "Here is laid the body of Jonathan Swift, Doctor of Divinity, Dean of this Cathedral Church, where fierce indignation can no longer rend the heart. Go, traveler, and imitate if you can this earnest and dedicated champion of liberty."

I focus on the phrase "where fierce indignation can no longer rend the heart."

Elsewhere in St. Patrick's Cathedral, a wooden door, dated to the fifteenth century, stands on display. The door once served as the entrance to the cathedral's chapterhouse—in medieval churches, an adjacent structure where the leaders of the church (mostly monks) would gather to legislate on cathedral business. At St. Patrick's today, little of the chapterhouse but the door remains. In the center of the door is a crudely cut hole.

The Irish expression "chancing the arm" means to take a risk. In cricket, broadcasters often use it when a batsman takes a chance and runs for an additional base. The expression actually originates at this damaged door.

But before I tell a story, first understand one meaning of the word "sanctuary."

Today, we sometimes hear of priests or ministers allowing illegal immigrants to live inside their churches to avoid authorities trying to deport them. A number of American churches in the 1980s tried to offer such "sanctuary" to illegal immigrants fleeing Central America, and in 2005 Senator Bennett from Utah introduced legislation on behalf of the Mormon Church allowing such immigrants to serve as church volunteers or missionaries.

This practice of granting sanctuary has a long tradition. In medieval times, the representative of secular law—in other words, the sheriff as the agent of the king—could not barge into a cathedral and arrest a person who had sought sanctuary. Sacred law forbade such an intrusion. The moment that person stepped out of the cathedral, he was back under the king's law.

In 1492, two famous Irish families were bitterly feuding with each other—the Ormonds and the Kildares. James Butler, Earl of Ormond, was forced to seek sanctuary in St. Patrick's Cathedral. Gerald Fitzgerald, Earl of Kildare, and his men besieged the chapterhouse where Butler was hiding. Several nerve-racking, terrible weeks passed. The two families worshipped the same God, they lived in the same community and even prayed at the same church, but they had grown to hate each other with such bitterness they were ready to kill each other.

We know our own hearts well enough to believe this is a true story.

No one now knows why, but for some reason, as the weeks passed, the aggressor Fitzgerald began to have a change of heart. He spent hours on his knees. "Later, go away," he answered those who interrupted his prayers and tried to reason with him. One day Fitzgerald stood outside the chapterhouse door and shouted to Sir James that, on his honor, he would not harm him if he came out of the chapterhouse. The Earl of Ormond, understandably so, said, "No, are you kidding?" Fitzgerald then did an odd thing, which became legendary. He took his spear and slowly hacked a hole in the middle of the door. When he had finished, he got down on his knees and thrust his arm through the hole, offering his hand, on his honor, to his enemy.

Imagine yourself in both men's positions. If you are the Earl of Kildare, Gerald Fitzgerald, you decide to risk your life by chancing the arm, pushing your hand through the hacked-out hole. If you are the Earl of Ormond, James Butler, your enemy has made himself totally vulnerable by blindly and foolishly sticking his hand through the opening. You can destroy this man you have hated if you wish.

It is easy to tear down, to feud, and hard, terribly hard—but essential—to build, or in this case, to forgive. In 1492 the Earl of Ormond decided to take the outstretched hand and shake it. He chose not war, but peace.

Consider two ironies to this story. The first is that no one remembers what the feud was about. Of course, I say, most reasons we fight with our friends or even go to war as a nation, after time passes, make no sense. Think about it. In a fight you had years ago—maybe even last month? last week?—why were you so angry? The second irony is that St. Patrick's Cathedral is also where one of the most famous graves in the world resides. Each of us, like Jonathan Swift, burns with fierce indignation, but usually not as champions of liberty for other people, but as human beings indignant about injustices done to ourselves. We usually seek revenge against others.

Can we find the moral courage to chance the arm? If we are given the hand to shake, do we have the moral courage to say yes?

And Miles to Go

In a rare breach of family etiquette, my son Evan has given me permission to tell a story in which he appears. One afternoon at Asheville School, a boarding school in North Carolina where we worked in the 1980s, my wife pulled Evan in his red wagon on their usual afternoon constitutional past the dormitories and baseball field, faculty houses and gardens, to the stables, where they watched the horses. A student I taught happened to be returning from the tennis courts and stopped to talk. He asked Evan where he was going. The little boy's answer was, "We have miles to go before we sleep."

The student took one look at Evan's mother and said, "That's the sickest thing I've ever heard."

Go back another ten years, to the 1970s. After a particularly hard day in the spring of my first year as a school administrator, at the Lovett School in Atlanta, I stood at the window of my office staring out at the school pond. I found myself, more than once, staring out that window at the pond—it was clearly the most beautiful place on campus. In her chair across the room, a senior—her name is Liza Wieland—read aloud the text from one of Pound's cantos. We were doing an independent study together. My mind—I'm sorry to say—was drifting. The words of the poem were in the air, but I couldn't catch them. My desk was overburdened. In those pre–e-mail days, at least fifteen pink telephone messages were piled atop each other. My Day-Timer had a to-do list the length of Homer's description of the Shield of Achilles. My assistant had interrupted our class four times with urgent messages.

Liza stopped and said, "You're staring out the window."

"I do that sometimes," I said.

"Do you love this work?" she asked.

I came awake. "Of course I love this job. Now let's get on with it. There's not much time left."

She didn't buy it. "Memorize these lines from Canto 81," she said. "Maybe they would help."

> What thou lovest well remains,
>   the rest is dross
> What thou lov'st well shall not be reft from thee
> What thou lov'st well is thy true heritage

A few days after my son Evan was born, an odd-sized package arrived in the mail. It was a beautiful child's picture book, inscribed to our son from my former student Liza Wieland, who is now a highly successful novelist and poet and chaired professor. Her letter said something like, "It can't hurt to start them young, and this poem is perfect for kids."

I am keenly aware that I risk groans from sophisticated lovers of poetry, but remembering the student and Evan's red wagon, you can guess. The poem was Robert Frost's "Stopping by Woods on a Snowy Evening." The famous last stanza reads,

> The woods are lovely, dark and deep,
> But I have promises to keep,
> And miles to go before I sleep,
> And miles to go before I sleep.

The gift explains my son's precociousness. And the poem is worth remembering. It tells a story we all understand. A man stops his journey on "the darkest evening of the year" to stare at the woods. You might remember now the image of staring. The man stops and stares. He watches the woods fill up with snow. They're lovely—delightful, pleasing, beautiful, and even worthy of love. They're dark, they're deep—resonant words if used well. His behavior is not normal. His behavior is not productive. It doesn't build a resume. It's not networking. His horse, whom I suspect is used to some hard driving, is so concerned "he gives his harness bells a shake." Yet former U.S. poet laureate Billy Collins describes the man as "engaged in a vital activity." Says Collins, "He is stopping to experience his own existence."

Imagine our students traveling on a long journey, miles and miles and miles, to borrow a Peter Townshend line. Consider this year's graduating class, now approaching the end of this part of the journey. They have suffered through the dark and cold of 9/11, of anthrax, an October sniper, and a war in Iraq, to keep the promises they've made. Think of all those promises. The final one of course is: I will graduate. But there were so many more. I will honor my father and mother. I promise to keep track of things. I will hold no other Gods before thee. I will put things back where they belong. I will not lie, cheat, or steal. I will keep an assignment notebook. I will learn to listen. I will learn how to read a textbook. I will stop clicking my eraser pencil. I will put away pogs and read *The Lion, the Witch and the Wardrobe*. I will do my science project. I will go on the eighth-grade camping trip and I will love it. I will join our Lower School head on Fridays to run off my punishment.

I promise to make use of my Upper School free time. I will not spend all my time playing Xbox. I will read thousands and thousands of pages. I will lift until it hurts, and then lift some more. I will sing in chapel. I will not download music onto the school computers. I will support other students. I will tuck my shirt in. I will shake hands with my opponents. I will write the best history term paper I can. I will get my application in on time. I will turn in my journal in the religion course. I will, I will, I will, and so on.

We value promises and believe in keeping them. It would be the worst kind of disingenuousness on my part to say we don't. We teachers and parents have done everything we can to keep our students' sleds moving.

But the man stopped. It was good that he stopped. He stared. The woods spoke to him—perhaps saying that what he loved well remains, that what he loved well was his true heritage. Then he was reminded again of his promises. Then he kept going.

We have spent most of our lives driving a sled and trying to figure out when to stop, when to watch the woods fill up with snow, and when to start the sled again. For long stretches of time, we have not been reflective about the journey but have driven the sled hard enough to realize that if we didn't stop and stare, we would crash the sled. I have very little advice to give our graduates other than to say that the sooner they can become deeply reflective about this yin and yang of life, this "drive-the-sled" and "stare-at-the-woods" of life, the better.

All our lives we struggle with our desires—to drive or stare? But even that either/or is simplistic. François Mauriac said we do not desire what we think we desire, and Tolstoy argued that the eternal error we make is in imagining that happiness is the realization of our desires. Thus, we need time between our desires, time to assess their frustration or their fulfillment, time to know what others think of our decisions, and time to think about how to weigh them in the future. Worshipping speed only makes us create thoughtless desires, and too many such desires lead to thousands of thoughtless promises, more promises than we can keep.

• 26 •

Our Man Micah

*I*n Ferguson, Missouri, the grand jury decided not to indict the police officer who shot Michael Brown. As we sat down to our Thanksgiving tables around the country, protests continued, fires were set, both the attorney general and the president spoke to the nation, our bishop and dean and the presiding bishop released statements, and national guard and police action continued. There were protests here in Washington, D.C., three days running.

Most of the prophet Micah's work is screeching lamentation and fierce condemnation of the people of his country. And when asked what is a better way to act, he answers: "To do justice, to love kindness, and to walk humbly with your God."

Each day we lose at something, but it hurts more, fiercely so, if you feel you lost because of injustice, because you were poor and not rich, or in a very few cases rich and not poor; black and not white, or in a few incidences white and not black; a woman and not a man, or in some cases a man and not a woman; Italian instead of Anglo-Saxon, or Anglo-Saxon instead of Irish, or Jewish instead of Gentile, or Palestinian instead of Jewish. The list, as you know, is endless and, in itself, debatable. Many of the injustices are real, but some are falsely perceived and flamed by hatemongers and press dramatists. We too often think we lose not because we lose in fair competition but because of the unfair advantages of the other.

We can swallow the consequences of loss if we feel we were treated fairly. "Fair and square" is our explanation: We lost "fair and square." But if we live in a group, a school, a nation, or world where some can't be given a square chance, we must work to right the wrong. Correct? We right the wrong not for negative reasons—to avoid riots or social explosions that in Washington, D.C., once raged on our now fashionable U Street or to keep the all-hallowed

88

financial markets from being closed—but for the positive reason of giving every human being in our society a chance to measure his or her worth by standards that are not terribly dissimilar from those of the people who breathe the same air. That is also, quintessentially, an American ideal.

Easy to say . . .

Which is why, I believe, our man Micah doesn't stop with justice alone. He knows, in the end, flawed human beings can't achieve perfect justice. And so justice needs a support system, a societal buy-in to any effort at justice, even a losing one. Micah argues we must love kindness.

"Kindness" has its etymological root in "kin," that is, in the relationships among human beings—we are kin, brothers and sisters. If you do not recognize that the people here, as well as the people in Ferguson, Missouri, or on the other side of the world, are by and large the same as you—having the same heart and lungs and mind and capacity for soul—you will not seek to do justice. We eliminate the kinship in the other person so we can justify being unkind. Thus in World War I we make a German into a Hun and justify killing him, except on Christmas Eve when much to the distress of the commanding generals the soldiers walk to the no man's land and sing Christmas Carols together, brother to brother. Today a terrorist in ISIS makes America into the Great Satan to kill Americans. And we are tempted to see ISIS as nonhuman, alien.

I was born into the Southern Baptist church, and I believe that most of the black Baptist ministers the weekend after the Ferguson decision spoke of the racial injustice at the heart of this country and its history, a reading I agree with. Many white Baptist ministers, at least in the Deep South, where I grew up and thus feel justified characterizing, more than likely defended the white police officer and the rule of law. I too insist on the rule of law. In my church of confirmation, most of the Anglican priests, who tend to be liberal, railed against the grand jury's decision, perhaps incorrectly. But they also railed against the terrible social ills visited on the black community by a power structure—the prosecutor and city council and police and the mayor, especially in Ferguson—that is all white. This is a crucial point to make, for city governments need to represent fairly the demographics of their people.

I make these points to show that as a citizen I find merit in arguments that a careless reporter, for simplicity's sake, might pit as opposites. I do this to demonstrate that Micah's first two admonitions cannot be separated from the third: to walk humbly with God.

Never forget that you can be in the presence of a person as earnest and committed to justice as you are, and he or she might stand across the witness table from you, fiercely disagreeing. You might be of different races, gender, and nationality. Micah does not only say walk humbly, though in itself that is great advice. He says walk humbly *with God*, which I believe is a reminder that the ultimate answers are ours to strive for but never to know fully. I know that for those of you who don't believe in God, you think I might be selling out. I don't. Anyone who has lived through at least two decades can document that the answer that seemed perfect twenty years ago doesn't seem flawless today. With age we learn we have no choice but to be humble about our wisdom. I am not saying become a political quietist—that is, someone, even a Christian, who takes no action for fear of taking wrong action. I am of the school that we argue and take what we believe are moral stances, right now, risk to ourselves, and we continue to work hard for justice all our lives. But we will be given glimpses of a perfect society and no more. Let us hope with Martin Luther King Jr. that the arc of the moral universe is long but bends toward justice.

In the meantime, be just, be kind, and be humble.

· 27 ·

The Prodigal Son

*N*arrative drive makes us ache to know what happens next. A younger son demands his inheritance and leaves home. He squanders his money and is forced to live with pigs. Then what? He goes straight back home to his father. How does his father make the ungrateful brat pay? He forgives him. He runs out and hugs him and throws a party in his honor. Is this the end? No, the older brother "blows a gasket." His father tries to convince him that he too should celebrate his younger brother's return. But we never find out whether the older brother can man up.

Sometimes a great story ends with an unanswered question, as if to ask, And you?

Great images resonate. Two in this story live. The first is a pigsty. The younger brother himself acted like the beasts he attended. He gorged himself without any thought to the future, but when his fortune was gone, he was left to snort and wallow. Starving, he envies even the pods the pigs are given to eat.

But "no one gave him anything."

The second image is the father running out to hug the son. One of Rembrandt's most famous paintings depicts the prodigal son kneeling before his father, only to be embraced by the man. In the Bishop's Garden beside the Washington National Cathedral stands a statue of the prodigal son and his father. Imagine, in fear and guilt, a powerful hug from someone who loves us nevertheless.

Boy leaves, boy lives in a different way than he did at home, boy returns home, and father and older brother respond. The story is also great because of the motivations of the characters. Are we intrigued by their choices? Do those choices ring true to our lives?

Let's catalogue the decisions.

The younger son is impatient and greedy. "Dad, I want my money now. I don't care what you say. I'm old enough now to handle it, you don't appreciate me, I don't need your advice, and I'm going to get it sooner or later, so cough it up." The younger son does not show understanding or patience and cannot extricate himself from his own greed and self-centeredness. Why imagine his father might have his own son's good at heart? Why think his father better suited to make the decision about when to deliver his inheritance?

The younger becomes dissolute. This is the meaning of prodigal—wasteful spending. The older brother later accuses the younger son of spending all his money on prostitutes. The boy could be whoring around, binge drinking, indulging himself in drug parties, running up debt, stealing, plagiarizing, and simply hiding behind one selfish lie after another until all of it is gone—money, health, and, most important, self-respect.

Sound like any kind of life you know?

All of us struggle with being prodigal. But all of us also are susceptible to a stroke of grace—my favorite line in the story is "he came to himself." Read again those simple words. "He came to himself." We are offered the opportunity to come to ourselves. And so the boy goes home, and because he recognizes not what he thinks he is but what he has truly become, he confesses.

Living through this story helps. This is what I believe most fathers, when they see a prodigal son coming down the road with his figurative tail between his legs, would say.

Father: "Here comes that disgusting ne'er-do-well. His mother and I have slaved all of our lives to provide him with the clothes on his back, with an education, and with an opportunity for the future, and that good-for-nothing has squandered it all. We have sacrificed for him, and he spat in our faces. Can you believe that little jerk has the gumption to come running home?"

And if the father has every reason to be upset, the older brother would not hold back either. Listen to what he might say: "All my life I've seen my parents favor my younger brother, the baby in the family, and he goes off to waste his inheritance while I stay here and work and obey. I keep the estate going. I help take care of things. My parents have never given me much of anything while they showered him with favors, and now he comes back home asking for more?"

We know in our hearts that we would struggle to forgive the younger brother. But the father runs toward him, hugs him, gives the boy a best coat and a fine party, and when the older brother can't make himself join them, the father tells his eldest that everything he has is also his brother's, if he would only understand. Truth is, the eldest might have imagined that he could have it all.

We want justice for ourselves, and we want to be the arbiters of that justice for ourselves and for others. The elder brother certainly thinks he has the right to both, and his bitterness is the result of his self-righteousness. Love and forgiveness trump even justice, or at least what we imagine as justice.

So think of this story when you gossip. Think of this story when you point your finger at someone else. Think of this story when you pass judgment on someone else who has behaved badly toward you or hasn't behaved as well as you yourself have behaved.

We must not care about keeping count, claiming justice, making comparisons and rankings. We can be free if we think it crucial to be compassionate about another person, knowing that we need his or her compassion in return. We can be free if we are more interested in celebrating what we have together than in pointing our fingers at what is wrong.

In short, we are the prodigal son but must strive to be his father.

VI

FACING FEAR

• 28 •

Anna and the Sniper

To acquire the habit of reading is to construct for yourself a
refuge from almost all of the miseries of life.

—W. Somerset Maugham

I began rereading *Anna Karenina* the second night of the sniper.

It was Thursday, October 3, 2002, the start of one of the most beautiful
months on the cathedral close, when the leaves in the Olmsted Woods turn
and the late roses in the Bishop's Garden quiver in the wind and the crisp blue
sky above the cathedral hints at eternity. The early morning news, however,
shocked us. In a northern suburb the night before, a man was mysteriously
shot while walking across a parking lot. Before those of us at school even
had time to imagine that awful event, in the next two hours an unidentified
sniper killed two men and two women. The deaths in Montgomery County,
Maryland, occurred close to schools we hold as friendly rivals, and the sniper's
pattern—if there was one—seemed to be heading south into the District toward us. At least that scenario seemed a possibility. For the next twenty-one
days, all we could think about was possibilities.

By the time I trudged upstairs that Thursday night to the bedroom, the
sniper had killed another man, this time in D.C. Six were dead in approximately twenty-four hours. I had talked for the seventh or eighth time with
Aggie Underwood, the headmistress of our sister National Cathedral School,
and we had shaped our plans to hold classes on Friday, October 4, but with
our campuses locked down. She and I promised to be back in touch after our
individual crisis teams had met early the next morning. Then we wished for
each other some sleep. No matter how bone-tired I was, though, I knew not
to try to sleep without first reading, for reasons every person over the age of
fifty understands.

I am blessed with a love of reading. While I have to be careful what I desire for all our boys without exception, I do think a love of reading unequivocally profits a person his entire life. Throughout September, I had been on a nonfiction binge, but somehow when I stood beside the bed, the events of the previous two days kept the most recent book of choice, a biography, closed on the night table. Perhaps I should have read a prayer manual. No one would question that choice. For me the answer was a novel. I needed to lose myself in a story. No matter how tragic its plot, no matter how troubled my own life, reading a great novel makes me feel keenly alive. It just so happened that a few weeks before, at the bookstore, I bought a new translation of Leo Tolstoy's *Anna Karenina*. What, read a novel about adultery, divorce, revenge, and suicide? Well, it's also about successful marital love, passion, and a good horse race. And since I fondly remembered the two separate times and places in my past when I had read that novel, I took it up a third time.

"All happy families are alike; each unhappy family is unhappy in its own way."

All of us as parents have worried about escapist tendencies in our children, wanting for them, when given the choice of fight or flight, more often than not, to choose to stand and fight. Don't hide, we say, put away childish things, engage—or even, be a man. I have suffered over young people I love wrapped in blankets in front of the television—to use one example of being completely disengaged—eating without any need for food, cocooning their brains with the violence and puerile wish fulfillment and nearly explicit sexual activity cable presents as common fare. Along with every other parent, I have wondered how much real anger and banging violence might be transferable to our own boys from the virtual games they escape into or the slickly deceptive movies they might believe to be real. And yet during the twenty-one October days locked in at school, while we had to suffer from the possibilities of all-too-real sniper attacks spinning through our heads, I was reminded that we cannot always choose to stand and fight. Sometimes flight is the wiser choice. After fighting the sniper crisis for as long as I could each day, I had to flee—straight home to locked doors and my family and then to the exquisite Anna.

We want our children to have what we know is necessary to life: a private world in which to escape. We must escape for both positive and negative reasons. When I began trying to write seriously, the master short story writer and my teacher Peter Taylor would encourage me by saying that fiction—an apparently escapist, unprofitable pursuit—is more true to reality than reality is to itself. We escape into a different world in a positive way if the world is imaginative, whatever the strange creatures of that imagination—toy soldiers, talking animals, monsters from outer space, counts and countesses from 1870s Russia. But children also need to escape for the negative reason that they must hide in a place that is anti-adult, to use a jarring phrase. We quickly understand that need when they are trying to hide from the harsh reality of evil lurking in nearby woods or parking lots, carrying a sniper's rifle. We understand that need far less when they are fleeing in order to survive us. To be specific, might not they flee the kind of father's moralistic tone evident in my comments about television and video games?

As parents we must be Janus-faced. We look into their private worlds, and we look away from them. We have to keep them from escaping completely from our guidance. They are the children we love, and they are not yet old enough to be left to their own devices (we pray in the confession of sins to be forgiven "the devices and desires of our own hearts"). We ask them about private, imaginative worlds that might traffic in the immoral: How are you using your computer? What Internet sites? What is that book, that magazine about? Is that the truth? We also ask them about their escapades: Who is being invited to this party and is anyone being purposefully left out? Who's driving? Who's in the car? What time? How are you checking in with me?

We must remind ourselves, however, that we also have to learn to look away, judiciously. We might not understand the imaginative choices our children make, preferring our own tastes to theirs (I always imagined that my daughter Emily, whom I love more than life, would have read all of George Eliot by the time she was fourteen. Needless to say . . .). We also don't need to know every conversation that occurs, to read all that is written, to write their papers, to complain their complaints to teachers, to eavesdrop or gossip or find out about them from other friends. The ultimate goal is to help them become independent of us.

I hold a highly public position but could not succeed at my work without a private life. A good portion of it is built around my imagination. I take nothing for granted, having lived long enough to realize all I hold close could dissolve tomorrow. Let us help our children learn to escape, both from the harsh realities of a sniper's world and from the smothering presence of their parents in their lives. If they find those healthy escapes, they will be more deeply responsible because their imaginations are keener. In time they will love us all the more because they will love us freely.

· 29 ·

Philip

$\mathcal{E}$very school suffers the loss of one of its own, but like Tolstoy's unhappy families, each loss is not alike.

On Friday morning May 15, 2015, the faculty gathered while three of us greeted the boys at carpool drop-off. Then the entire Lower School, grades four through eight, assembled in the silence of the Little Sanctuary for the start of a day like no other. I could say little: An arsonist had set a fire in the home of one of our youngest students. The police couldn't yet identify the bodies beyond "three adults and one juvenile." But all of us knew, without my having to say, that Philip had stayed home on Thursday, still suffering a concussion from his go-kart accident. If he were safe, surely we would have heard.

It was only the start of difficult questions unanswered by the horrifying details revealed over the next few days.

The chaplains said prayers for the dead, for the safety of the sisters who were away from home at boarding schools, and for the entire community, both at our school and on the cathedral close. Our Lower School head spoke briefly about Philip. Our academic dean, a psychologist himself, talked about grieving and sent the older grades to different locations throughout the school, where they would sit with their teachers and one of our counselors or chaplains. Throughout, the bishop of Washington was with us. And then we planned to return to a modified routine, with lots of recess and with each boy knowing that he could opt in or out, however he felt at the time.

The three classes of Philip's grade stayed with us, on the first two rows of the sanctuary. Nine adults found our way among forty nine- and ten-year-olds, with our chaplain and dean helping them to sit in silence or talk. I sat to the side and at an angle, so that I could see each boy's face, so that I could be ready to help in any way, though I had no earthly idea what that way might be. I too suffered the loss; I was at a loss. We had cautioned ourselves not to let our adult affect impose on the boys—yes, it was all our grief, adult and child, but Philip was their buddy, their speed demon, their friend, and for some their go-to guy.

One boy—tiny, clouded eyes—said he was sad and dropped his face on his teacher's lap. His entire body shook. She rubbed his back. Another boy said he was scared. We assured him he was safe. Later, he would say to a counselor that Philip's parents probably said the same thing to him.

"I'm angry," another boy said.

Adult heads nodded.

"He was so upbeat on our baseball team. He didn't get mad at anyone but encouraged us."

"When he was in class on Tuesday, I liked how we tried to keep quiet for his concussion."

A long-time teacher stood to remember losing another fourth grader near the start of his career. "I think about him every day." He sat down and wept.

Another boy leaned into the arms of the librarian, tears streaking his chubby face. "I couldn't sleep. I tried to read the Bible."

One of the boys I know better than many others looked on in complete silence. He always said hello and shook my hand, smiled, and asked about my day. Later, when we spread large sheets of paper out on the floor of their classroom, he would draw Philip's go-kart, but with fifteen seats.

"For all of us," he said.

He didn't say much more for another two days, but he kept drawing representations of Philip's soul.

Another boy said he hoped to win a trophy over the weekend and set it down next to Philip's grave. He looked directly at me. "I mean, when he has one."

And there were adult words—we couldn't help ourselves. It's OK, however you feel. Don't feel guilty about whatever you do today, however you feel. Grief comes and goes, for a long time. It shows itself in different ways. Sometimes you don't know that you're feeling grief. Or fear. Or sadness. Or anger.

In time the boys grew tired. We suggested they go outside. Run around, sit and talk, play games—it didn't matter. It was a beautiful day and they needed to stop sitting and talking. But our great Lower School head, forty-four years of working with young boys, suggested that before we went outside, we move from the first two rows of the sanctuary up to the altar table and the great stained glass window behind it.

Most of the time, one boy observed, the light streaming through the stained glass window was red. Their earliest chapel period was 10:30 a.m., and sometimes they were in the building later than that. But it was only 8:45 in the morning, and the early light from the east over downtown Washington played primarily through the blue pieces in the glass. I don't know what to make of that other than I was surprised a boy noted it and the others agreed. We gathered all forty boys around the altar table, two to three deep, the adults on the perimeter. I was stunned. For me, it was the passage of time. We were one week from the commencement for boys who were eighteen years old, at the end of their journey at St. Albans. I imagined that nine years hence these boys would be young men and they might gather around that table again before they graduate, look into each other's eyes, and remember their friend Philip.

I did not attend the last Lower School chapel of the year. Its tradition has our fifth-grade teacher, such a master at photography he could make a career of his talent, present a slide show of the best shots he had taken during the entire school year, a walk down memory lane at a time in life when nine months feels like a long haul. Every year he makes certain that every boy in the five grades of the Lower School has at least one photograph of him in the show (all teachers reading this smile at the necessity of this detail). Traditionally I don't attend this chapel, caught up in preparation for the events of commencement, but I had been a part of the discussions about whether or not to include a photo of Philip. Ultimately, I was told: my call.

Yes. Don't finish with Philip but just include him in the routine photos of the comings and goings of a school year.

The photos were a success. The chapel service had students and teachers talking, but for an unexpected reason.

Our Little Sanctuary is one of the oldest buildings on the Washington National Cathedral close and is still not air-conditioned. Originally built as an office for Bishop Satterlee, the founding bishop of the cathedral, and as a storing tank, so to speak, for iconic structures such as the Canterbury Pulpit, which would be moved into the cathedral nave once it was built, it was imagined to be a short-lived place. The boys grew too fond of it over the years, and now it's iconic in their hearts and souls. None of my predecessors has been willing to raise the money to modernize a place that isn't full of people for much of the day. Thus during the late spring and early fall we keep the windows and doors open and have standing fans that help to cool the place, especially when 220 fourth through eighth graders pack into it, mid-morning, at the end of May. During the construction of a new academic building, we turned the Little Sanctuary into a daily classroom and hung a drop-down screen beneath the rood cross above the altar. After we finished, the chaplains decided to leave it up, for services just like this last one of the school year.

The boys did well, disciplining their "we're-almost-finished" rowdiness, and at the beginning of the service they kept silence. They led the prayers. Then they moved into a half-reverence of sorts, for soon they'd laugh and cheer at the year's worth of photos chronicling their lives.

As the photos began, a goldfinch flew through the open window and perched on the bar that held up the screen, directly above the photos as if to get the best view in the house. For a long time it did not fly away. And then, for another long time it did not fly away. It did not fly away until the slide show was completely over and the boys clapped furiously. It flew out the opposite window from where it entered. In one way, out the other.

Sometimes I preach about "seeing as believing" and "believing as seeing." Do we believe something because we see it, or do we see something because we believe it?

Wow, about the bird, there was a flurry of call and response among the students and the teachers. The Lower School chaplain told me everyone noticed and some sat there with open mouths, stunned. It was gorgeous. It never left. It looked like it was watching. A number of boys asked the chaplain if she saw it and if she could explain why it was there. A sixth-grade teacher had his boys return to class and wrote a prompt on the board: The Bird. They wrote without pause for twenty to thirty minutes. The chaplain is well versed in Native American spirituality, which apparently includes beliefs that souls can move into birds for a number of days after death.

"I am absolutely convinced," she said, "Philip was with us."

I can't begin to know all the religious and literary allusions to birds and spirituality. When I heard this story, I immediately recalled the emotions I have felt sometimes in the presence of an unexpected bird—the sudden visitation, the head that turns as if to speak to me, the resonance of the color—and because I do read a lot I remember the literary bird that has meant a good deal to me in the course of my life. It's an ancient text, from the Venerable Bede:

> The present life of man . . . is like to the swift flight of a sparrow through the room wherein you sit . . . whilst the storms of rain and snow prevail abroad; the sparrow, I say, flying in at one door, and immediately out at another, whilst he is within, is safe from the wintry storm; but after a short space of fair weather, he immediately vanishes out of your sight, into the dark winter from which he had emerged. So this life of man appears for a short space, but of what went before, or what is to follow, we are utterly ignorant.

I know my life, however blessed, is swift enough. Philip's was taken from him—from all of us—too quickly.

VII

GREAT SCHOOLS, GREAT PRIVILEGE

· 30 ·

Harvard or Heaven?

The end of education is to enable our boys—and ourselves—to live usefully, richly, fully—today and every day. This purpose, worked at earnestly, patiently, and humbly, in the spirit of the Teacher Jesus Christ, who has done some unusual things with human beings, will allow us to see college admission and all the impedimenta of living in their proper perspective.

—Canon Charles Martin, *Letters from a Headmaster's Study*

*H*ere's a quiz question. For four months and one day I've been on the job, and I have informally tracked what people say to me most frequently. I don't mean what they say to me personally, that is, all the wonderful and cascading concern about how my children are adjusting to school. I mean instead, What do people say to me, over and over again, about being headmaster of St. Albans?

Some of you might now be thinking that people offer advice, freely offer advice, freely offer abundant advice, and you might even be running through your mind now deciding which piece of advice tops the chart. I'm happy to say advice is not the answer—at least not the explicit answer. Occasionally I have heard sentences that begin, "Whatever you do, don't . . ." Dot. Dot. Dot. "Whatever you do, don't miss the House Tour, or don't mess with the refectory." "Whatever you do, don't go co-ed, don't change chapel." "Whatever you do, don't lose to Landon in lacrosse." "Whatever you do, don't answer the phone if Aggie Underwood [my counterpart at our sister school] is rip-snorting mad."

No, what I have heard most often is not an imperative sentence, but a declarative sentence. To be more precise, I have been repeatedly asked if I've heard one certain declarative sentence. I have indeed heard the sentence; I guess I've heard it one hundred times or more, most often of course at St. Albans or from the Canterbury Pulpit in the cathedral, but also in places far and wide: while I was squeezing a cantaloupe at Safeway, before I cut into a double-chocolate cheesecake in a downtown restaurant, and even beneath the orangutan line at the zoo. Talk about a legacy to live up to: If you happen to sight the seventh headmaster, ask him if he's heard what Canon Martin, the fourth headmaster, said—what he famously said.

Most recently, because even I realize I'm onto something here, I've asked, "OK, when did Canon Martin say this? Did he write it in one of his letters from the headmaster's study?"

"Well, you see," one person said, "there was this father whose son didn't get into Harvard, and he stormed into Canon Martin's study and said he had paid all this St. Albans tuition for nothing, absolutely nothing." And Canon Martin answered him with the famous sentence. Or another person said, "Well, you see, all these parents whose children got into the most selective colleges in the country were crowing about their super bright sons and how great St. Albans was, and Canon Martin interrupted them to say . . ." I've also heard he said it in his chapel talks, to the faculty, in his lectures after lunch, and whenever the occasion moved him, thank you very much. The only story I haven't heard is that he said it to his bulldog Cleopatra.

The reports about the first part of the famous sentence are unreliable. Some people say, "The mission of St. Albans," while others say, "St. Albans exists to," and still others take the simplest and quickest way to the end by beginning, "St. Albans prepares." The gist of this one-sentence school legacy is always the same: "St. Albans prepares boys not for the kingdom of Harvard, but for the kingdom of heaven."

Now, before many people get their boola-boola hackles up, let me quickly say that when Canon Martin said "Harvard," he of course meant "highly selective colleges." Out of interest and necessity, then, since arriving at St. Albans, I have meditated on this oft-repeated sentence about Harvard and heaven and what it means to us now. Its rhetorical power fascinates me almost as much as its meaning, for, as Francis Bacon said, its rhetoric makes it able "to contend." It begins with a declaration: St. Albans prepares boys. Subject, active verb, direct object. It is, like Canon Martin himself, muscular, and its force is then met by the most forceful of words—"not." We know those "nots" from the Ten Commandments. The naysayer "not" then parallels our two key words, "Harvard" and "heaven," the first capitalized but the second not, and each is linked together by the profound and repeated word "kingdom."

Be patient with me here: As an English teacher, I can't resist. Canon Martin's Bible is King James's Bible, the Authorized Version. When Christ says, "Let the dead bury their dead," his first "dead" differs in meaning from the second "dead," just as Canon Martin's first "kingdom" is nevertheless meant to differ from the second "kingdom." And of course, the entire sentence is built around the very first words Christ speaks in the Gospel of Mark: "The time is fulfilled, and the kingdom of God is at hand" (Mark 1:15). And look what else the sentence does. It first introduces the word "kingdom" with Harvard. That is not a phrase easily recognizable—the kingdom of Harvard—but as soon as you hear it, you nod (perhaps laugh) and say, "yes, that's fitting," and then because of that yes-saying, Jesus' crucial and well-known phrase "kingdom of heaven" rings out all the more powerfully. (St. Matthew, by the way, because of his sacred reverence for the word "God" and his refusal to speak it aloud, unlike the other gospel writers, generally used the phrase "kingdom of heaven" instead of "kingdom of God.") Finally, just listen to the sounds of the words, Harvard and heaven, the first kingdom with the repetition of the hard *ar* sounds on either side of the middle *v*—Har-vard (that is, if you choose to pronounce the *r*s in the word not as *h*s)—followed in the second word by the softer and repeated sounds on either side of the *v* in "hea-ven." One kingdom of this world, one kingdom of the next: hard and concrete, soft and spiritual. St. Albans prepares for the latter.

But is that true? Really true? And now you smile slightly or guffaw. If you hear enough people say the same thing enough times, you begin like Hamlet's mother to wonder if they protest too much. In a wonderful poem, "So I Said I Am Ezra," A. R. Ammons writes, "As a word too much repeated falls out of being." I have no doubt, of course, that Canon Martin meant what he said, but I have this suspicion, based on the wisdom of having our cake and eating it too, that what many of us really mean to say is, "St. Albans prepares boys not for the kingdom of Harvard, nor for the kingdom of heaven, but for both!"

Throughout St. Albans' history, academic excellence has indeed been a primary value. It remains so. We embrace that goal and in fact propose that intellectual excellence and high performance are not mutually exclusive from spiritual understanding. Jesus Christ—the great artist of parables—did not say, "It is easier for a camel to enter the eye of a needle than for a smart man to get into heaven."

But we do need to reassert our first values. Here and now. In a world and in particular a country where far too many of us desire not simply Harvard but a value-added Harvard, that is, the right college weighed, measured, and used to bring on the right firm or practice, whose purpose is to earn money for the right vacation home and the right pre-preschool for the children and the right church for the holiday season, we must once more assert the radical primacy of the kingdom of heaven and all it symbolizes in our lives.

But Harvard is a concrete place, supposedly offering a lifetime of prestige, and the kingdom of heaven is anything but. Long-time St. Albans teacher John C. Davis told me that one student, upon hearing Canon Martin say one too many times that he wanted to get students into the kingdom of heaven, responded, "But when is the director of admissions going to visit?" I am not a theologian but a teacher, and I feel comfortable taking on the "kingdom of heaven" phrase only as it relates to our school and the ethical and spiritual life of our community. And I know I can best speak about the kingdom of heaven through story.

In the Book of Genesis, Jacob, I remind you, was not a perfect boy. He was a trickster, a mama's boy who dwelled in tents, bought Esau's birthright, and conspired with his own mother to deceive his blind father and steal his older twin's blessing. He was such a mess that, after five chapters of Genesis, his blessing and good luck become a curse, and he falls into despair. Then he prays for the grace of God: "I am not worthy of the least of all Thy mercies." He camps on the riverside and decides that the next morning he will face up to his aggrieved brother Esau: In other words, he will accept responsibility for his life. This is where my picture of the kingdom of heaven begins. We must teach young men that however successful buying and conspiring and deceiving and stealing might seem to be, in the end they will need to rely on mercies beyond their understanding, to convert their false fears about life into right action, and cross the river to exchange the blessings of this life with their brothers and sisters.

Oh that it would be so simple. Jacob sends the others away, and Genesis simply says, "And Jacob was left alone, and there wrestled a man with him until the breaking of the day." Please note the man was a mystery—a stranger, perhaps a demon. Jacob simply didn't know. What we hope for all of us at St. Albans, all who gather in our great cathedral, all of humankind, is that when the disguised angel grabs hold and starts to hurt us, we wrestle with all our might and don't let go. It's easier to let go. It's so much easier to let go. It's easier to lie than to tell the truth, to steal than to give, to cheat than to make the grade our work deserves, to be selfish than to serve, to buy than to resist, to disbelieve than to believe, to despair than to hope, to turn from the river crossing and go back, to take the easy wrong over the hard right. But we want to hold on even through injury until whomever we're wrestling with relents, becomes an angel of God, and says, "Thy name is no more Jacob but Israel." The kingdom of heaven is in the daily wrestling for personal ethics and the shared ethics of an entire community like St. Albans, and the kingdom of heaven is in the name-changing blessing God gives to us, so that we can cross the river, then and every day, and share that blessing with others.

May the God of Jacob made Israel and our Lord Jesus Christ, who wrestled with Satan in the wilderness and was then ministered to by angels, vouchsafe blessings upon this school and upon us all, so that all people, and in particular both the Church and the Commonwealth of this land, may benefit by our wrestling labors.

· 31 ·

What Wakes You Up
in the Middle of the Night?

When I lie down I say, "When shall I rise?"
But the night is long,
and I am full of tossing until dawn.

—Job 7:4 (NRSV)

The question can come in odd places, at odd times: on the sideline of a child's soccer match, at a cocktail party, over a shared meal. "What wakes you up in the middle of the night?" is, more than likely, a well-meaning question, a reach for friendship. Dangerous, though, isn't it? The friend we ask might answer truthfully.

Because of my job, I am often asked this question. I admit that anxieties feast on the job of ring-mastering a school, but every job, regardless, must cope with anxiety. Many more jobs than mine have greater anxieties to manage, and in Washington, D.C., in particular, some jobs are even beset by the raging anxieties of the entire world. Perhaps of greatest significance, in any job the mind can make a hell of heaven. All this having been said, most people who ask me this question assume, I believe, that I wake up worried that St. Albans won't blow the top off our upcoming campaign, that one or more of our boys will do something dangerously stupid in the middle of the night, or that the terrorist threat lurking about Washington will one unsuspecting moment bite our heads off.

Pray God—let none of that happen. Or, pray God, let not happen—even worse—what I can't imagine!

All of us hope the institutions we love can survive both perceived and real threats. All of us know that the human beings who people an institution are resilient. I tread on shifting sand, then, when I propose that my greatest

111

anxiety is that, during my tenure, something far more subtle happens. St. Albans will give up struggling for its soul.

Let me explain why I believe the sand shifts beneath me when I say this. In my mind's ear, I hear my friends (and some enemies, to be truthful), who, at times, are cynics. "Come on, headmaster," they say, "that's such headmaster blarney. An institution does not have a soul. You're telling me you don't worry more about raising money, the damage that a drunken boy can do to himself and innocent others, or terrorism than some obligatory, sanctimonious, and clichéd notion of a school's soul?"

Yes, of course, I do lose sleep over these concerns, as a parent and as a headmaster. But we can and will face them, and will struggle to soldier on, trying to be stronger as a community, deeper as contemplatives. We have a hundred years of perspective to summon. But I do believe communities develop a common soul. Lose that, and what profit to us are endowments and awards and buildings, Gothic and otherwise?

Perhaps carelessly I equate a manmade institution with a mortal life, in which the divine soul lives until and beyond death. An educational institution is also mortal, of course, but unlike our human being's three score and ten, no average life expectancy frames a school. For example, one of our namesakes, St. Albans School of Hertfordshire (north of London), has recently celebrated its millennium. At the other end of the scale, how many charter schools in this city have in the last five years opened their doors and already closed them? However tenuous the connection might be, though, I nevertheless want to pose that a school, modern or ancient, has its own kind of soul.

Last month I finished a novel by Pat Barker, *Double Vision*, in which one of the main characters, a recent widow, makes the following observation about a priest. "The trouble was, Kate thought, that Alec always thought of himself as a good man. That made him sound smug and horrible, which he wasn't, but he did tend to assume that in the great war of good and evil he'd always be on the right side, whereas Kate couldn't help thinking real adult life starts when you admit the other possibility." When I first read this, I thought about my own spiritual immaturity, for I do imagine myself always on the right side. But then I thought about the school I head and realized that the besetting sin can apply to us collectively, also, so that, however kind Kate might be to us, we come out sounding "smug and horrible." This is especially true for a place like St. Albans—one hundred years old, bred by Episcopal pomp and circumstance, birthed by the nation's cathedral, steeped in male privilege, nestled atop a mountain named St. Alban overlooking the nation's capital ("My gawd," the cynic says).

I am deeply proud of everything we do right. We teach integrity, service, excellence, compassion, and charity, and we try to act in a consistent way that narrows the gap of hypocrisy between word and deed. But our soul suffers if we, like Alec in the novel, identify deceit, pride, shoddiness, and hatred and assume that, pressed to choose, we will always decline and instead be in the right. Then in that "great war of good and evil" we have capitulated to the enemy. So do I worry more about our school's soul than raising money, struggling with a boy's mistakes, or safeguarding against a terrorist threat? Let me turn the question. I profoundly believe that how we inspire people to give, not simply their money but their lives, and how we discipline and counsel a young man who has gone astray for whatever reason, and how we learn to trust God to determine our start and end times are essential measures of a school's worth—in other words, its soul.

As for what wakes me up in the middle of the night, what could be worse for our school than saying, when it comes to anxieties about ourselves, that we have none?

· 32 ·

What Benefits Our Labors

The responsibility and opportunity of St. Albans, independent
of community and state, free from passing fads and fashions, is
to hold to some values of the past, to search restlessly for truth
in the present, and to maintain a community in which a student
can develop his own distinctive individuality.

—Canon Charles Martin, *Letters from a Headmaster's Study*

*R*ead some journalistic news from a recent political season:

Prep schools are luscious targets for ridicule; their graduates sometimes
seem frightfully predictable. Yet the schools thrive even now. In this most
egalitarian of societies, we cling to some of the trappings of class distinc-
tions. Even at the pinnacle of our democracy.

This snippet from a *Washington Post* piece by Marc Fisher, along with a
number of editorials and opinion pieces from around the world, became part
of my daily mail when alumnus Al Gore entered the 2000 presidential race.
I am certain Barbara Chase, head of school at Phillips Academy in Andover,
Massachusetts, alma mater of George W. Bush, had a similar experience.
The presidential election spotlighted our schools and the raison d'être of all
prep schools. The costs of attending prep schools always raise questions of
class in our society, whether or not a political race calls attention to the issue.
But in this longest and costliest of presidential campaigns, both candidates
were scions who decided to speak at much greater length about their small
hometowns in Tennessee and Texas than they did about their thriving and
expensive prep schools outside Boston and "inside the Beltway."

Not every journalist, however, has ridiculed prep schools, nor attacked
St. Albans in particular. Some in fact praised Canon Martin for shaping

the moral lives of two generations of young men, including the Democratic candidate for president and two brothers of the Republican candidate. Others recognized the school's preeminent teachers. They recalled John Davis's emphasis on superior intellectual standards, the Rev. Craig Eder's nurturing of the spirit, Ferdinand Ruge's insistence on clear writing, and Dean Stambaugh's masterful teaching of the arts. But all of us know that great teaching for a few boys is not best-selling political news.

What makes news is fashion, privilege, and power. One magazine spoke of the swimming pool, where "in classless America, St. Albans lets riff-raff . . . use the pool when the school is closed . . . and [one] can . . . [listen to] the hiss of well-connected Georgetown ladies dishing the dirt." Another said that the graduates of prep schools like St. Albans are "perfectly comfortable with the notion everything revolves around . . . their ambition." Another writer said St. Albans still suffers from the "vestigial belief that young people can and must be molded into leaders" and the "now unfashionable idea of noblesse oblige." In fact the most frequent phrase used among all the articles I have read is "noblesse oblige," the late-fifteenth-century phrase that suggests, to be succinct, that privilege entails responsibility.

A remarkable idea, this.

Phillips Academy, Andover, was founded in 1778. At its beginning, it worked to provide a Calvinist education that trained minds and built character, which included inculcating the ideals of social usefulness in its students. Andover's constitution reads as follows: "Goodness without knowledge is weak; knowledge without goodness is dangerous; both united form the noblest character, and lay the surest foundation of usefulness to mankind." Harriet Lane Johnston's gift to create St. Albans was made in 1903; the school opened its door as an Episcopal cathedral choir school in 1909. Every philosophy statement written since the school's founding has spoken of its central tenet of building moral character in boys (the hard right over the easy wrong) so that they can be useful and "both the Church and the Commonwealth of this land may benefit by their labors."

Every college preparatory school—whether it was founded last year in California, or sits on the hill overlooking our nation's capital, or has a 222-year history in New England—must squarely face up to charges that it is elitist, that it is part of an unjust class system that rewards the privileged and powerful at the expense of the poor, and that its ideas are outmoded. We cannot let those who make these criticisms, however, some of whom are prep school graduates themselves, frame the argument in self-righteous terms of "we are egalitarian and you are not." I have always believed that independent schools in this country, when faced with these accusations from the so-called egalitarians, sidestep the central issue by citing their financial aid budgets as a way to prove that plenty of children who attend independent schools are not rich. That is an important statement, which I second. Nevertheless, 72 percent of the children in this independent school still come from families who pay the full tuition.

My defense is built around the idea of choice and of responsibility. Let's state the bald truth about the egalitarian attack, here at the "pinnacle of our democracy," as the writer I first cited has written. While this is a country founded on the principle of the equality of humankind, that equality means equal rights, equal responsibilities, and equal treatment under the law. It does not mean equal distribution of goods. Any citizen who is blessed with more material goods than most nevertheless has a legal obligation to pay taxes in support of the commonwealth and a moral obligation to abide by the law and to work for the common good. That citizen may choose to use his or her income to educate a child in a private school, as long as that citizen pays taxes in support of public education and the school of choice doesn't discriminate against any class of citizens.

What, then, is the obligation of a school that does not accept money from the government but instead accepts money from those citizens fortunate enough to spend beyond their school taxes on the education of their own children? I have some firm beliefs. A school must explain to the people who support it that a portion of the school's money—whether it be from tuition, gifts, or endowment—goes to support a financial aid fund. That fund makes it possible for students who meet all the admission standards other than the ability to pay the entire amount to attend the school. Many school people don't want to say this because they don't want to remind people that their gifts might be supporting someone else's child. I want to say this, for along with many other kinds of diversity, this economic diversity is essential in creating the right tone for educating children. It's obviously not the same experience as a public school classroom, but it is also not the same experience as a classroom in a school where there is no financial aid. During the 2000 presidential election, the journalists listed the sons of the famous at our school. No one profiled any of the young men who were on financial aid, whose education at St. Albans won them admission and even scholarships to the most selective colleges in the country, who have excelled at careers in academia and law and theater and even journalism and politics, and who are deciding to send their own children to St. Albans or schools very similar to ours.

Our second obligation as a school is not to mistake admissions selectivity for elitism. An independent school must guard against becoming an adjunct to social or country clubs that serve very different purposes in our society than the education of the young. While it is the obligation of a head of school to raise money for an institution and thus spend time with people who have the wherewithal to ensure a school's future, he or she must push to include as many people as possible in fund-raising and never mistake that essential function as anything but groundwork for the education of children. The true art is in making certain the young are taught well and taught that "nobility" in our democracy should have more to do with discernment than investment portfolios.

Also, the word "social" in a school should not be connected most frequently in the students' minds with Mom and Dad's money or proms or parties but with the concept of service and the effort to be connected with others and useful to them. School spirit, in fact, should first of all be an internal phenomenon, in that we should have the kind of spirit that serves one another and then leads us to serve the wider community. I don't disagree with the critics who say social service can be accompanied by condescension, but does that mean schools shouldn't try to teach this civic duty because it might get delivered with human flaws? I gladly use the words "usefulness" and "obligation" and "duty," and I use them without any hesitation.

I perfectly well understand that a person can't run for president and spend a lot of time talking about life at Andover or St. Albans. But the ideals of both institutions are not outmoded. Any institution that has been working to teach young people that goodness without knowledge is weak and knowledge without goodness is dangerous is a school to be admired. St. Albans has its flaws, but we will continue to teach young men that from whatever economic background they come, it is a privilege to be educated here. With this privilege of a St. Albans education, and with whatever privileges they gain from their family background, they must recognize that they have the responsibility to serve. And if that service takes the form of leadership, so be it.

• 33 •

An Authoritative Community

Only connect!

            —E. M. Forster, *Howards End*

The catalogue of ills sounds like the stuff of talk shows: rising rates of depression, anxiety, attention deficit, conduct disorders, and thoughts of suicide—the afflictions of serious mental, emotional, and behavioral problems. What's worse, while medications and psychotherapies might help, they can't cure the illnesses. Neither can special programs for the "at-risk." The crisis is clearly defined and well documented: The mental and behavioral health of children in the United States is deteriorating.

Here's the thesis of the 2003 Commission on Children at Risk, a group of thirty-three children's doctors, research scientists, and mental health and youth service professionals, convened by the YMCA of the USA, Dartmouth Medical School, and the Institute for American Values: The crisis in American childhood comes from a lack of connectedness—first, to other people; second, to moral and spiritual meaning. Neuroscientists increasingly believe that the human child is "hardwired to connect," not only *to* other people, but also *for* moral meaning and openness to the transcendent. Connectedness is best learned from groups of people, that is, social institutions, organized around certain purposes. Many of these institutions have disappeared in the lives of children.

What's the solution? Authoritative communities (with your indulgence, let me caution you not to mistake "authoritative" for "authoritarian"). The people in authoritative communities are committed to one another over time, and they model and pass on at least part of what it means to be a good person and to live a good life. Renewing broken communities and building new ones are the key environmental changes necessary to improve the lives of children in this country.

St. Albans should bear witness to the power of an authoritative community. The moment I express such a hope, however, I must recognize that for one hundred years, even as decade by decade our admissions have expanded the school's reach racially, culturally, and socio-economically, we nevertheless have had the privilege of choosing the boys who enter our community. Most communities have no such advantage. We have also been blessed with good fortune, teachers who see their work as a vocation, exceptional students and families, a beautiful cathedral close, and, many more years than not, financial stability. Sustaining a good community, however, even with our privileges, is not easy. But working at it affords us a chance to make a profound contribution to the public life of our city and our country. As we employ the benefits of an authoritative community, we teach young men not simply how to be moral and well-educated citizens, but also how to engage in the public debate about the advantages of such communities for all peoples.

What, then, is an authoritative community? The Commission on Children at Risk describes a community that desires to foster a child's need to connect. The authoritative community should be a warm, nurturing, multigenerational social institution that includes children. While it establishes clear limits and expectations, it treats children as ends in themselves and sustains, on their behalf, a long-term focus. The core of its work is performed largely by non-specialists. It reflects and transmits a shared understanding of what it means to be a good person. It encourages spiritual and religious development. Finally, it is philosophically oriented to the equal dignity of all persons and to the principle of love of neighbor.

The description is compelling. It can guide communities as small as families to think about how they live together. It can certainly guide large communities like schools to examine their practices. At St. Albans, for example, it calls the people in this community to know each other, to respect each other, and to connect. Anonymity is not allowed. We must build those connections over more than one generation: The most senior of our faculty was born before the 1929 crash, and the C Formers (fourth graders) do not know what a rotary dial is. We also must continue to tout generalists, for even with the explosion of the number of "support personnel" in schools, we want teachers not only to know their subject area deeply but to contribute in more than one way. They teach, they advise, they coach, they sponsor, and, most important, they listen. We also believe boys should connect to more than one pursuit. They will have plenty of time in long careers to gain specialized expertise. At this time in their lives, they must not concentrate on merely one thing.

The description of an authoritative community also reminds us how essential the law is for children. We use it to establish clear limits and expectations, with real consequences for actions that work against the community. But as human beings who have all fallen short of the law, we must also be warm, nurturing, and especially forgiving, knowing perfectly well that adolescent boys will make our same mistakes. And as we work with young men to teach them to take responsibility for their actions, we explain to them that we embrace the idea of forgiveness because of our religious mission built on the great commandments of loving God and neighbor. Spiritual development will slowly come as a boy lives in the law, loves his neighbor, and forgives both himself and his neighbor for falling short. He should see it is a lifelong quest.

Finally, we must resist the temptation to use the brilliance and accomplishments of our boys as reflections of our status as a school or as a family or as a parent. We must remind, counsel, encourage, and cajole ourselves, both as parents and teachers, to refrain from using children as ends for ourselves. Our moral task, then, is to teach our children to discover who they are as they struggle each day with the human need to connect and the paradoxes of their own desires and our expectations. This means that day after day we don't loom over them or push back too hard but stay firmly by their side, helping them to search through the apparent boredom of the mundane or the confusion of contemporary life for a divine clue to who they truly are—maybe in a word that strikes their soul, maybe with an arm around their shoulder, or maybe simply in the silence of being alone. In helping them to make such connections, then, we must discipline ourselves to take a long view. As teachers, we are fortunately positioned to take such a long view because our job is to prepare the boys, whom we love and cherish, not to stay but to leave. A few years later, if they were educated in the right kind of community, they show up again, but the awkward has become graceful, the crude refined, the shy articulate, and even the hater now a lover. These magical transformations best happen if the spell is first cast in an authoritative community.

VIII

TEACHING

· 34 ·

Silas Marner and Me

> By the time Eppie was three years old, she developed a fine
> capacity for mischief, and for devising ingenious ways of being
> troublesome, which found much exercise, not only for Silas's
> patience, but for his watchfulness and penetration. Sorely was
> poor Silas puzzled on such occasions by the incompatible de-
> mands of love.
>
> —George Eliot, *Silas Marner*

*M*iss Purdy had arranged the desks in our classroom to form a *U* so that
she possessed a direct line of sight between her desk and every ninth-grade
student. Did she know something funny was going on?

On that day in 1965, we had spent most of our English class discuss-
ing why Silas Marner had become a miser, but as was her habit, Miss Purdy
decided near the conclusion of class that we needed an extra chapter to read
for homework. She finished the discussion ten minutes early and told us to
get started.

"And don't accuse me of never giving you a break," she said.

Instead of grading papers, however, she sat very still at her desk. I grew
suspicious. Slyly I watched her as she watched each one of us open our texts
and apparently lose ourselves in the story that fifty years ago was a staple of
the English curriculum and today is nearly forgotten. I read the same sentence
in *Silas Marner* over and over, however, for nine of the allotted ten minutes.
It was the first but not the last time in my life I wished I had eyes on each
side of my face, like a horse or a fish, so that, without any movement of my
head my left eye could watch Miss Purdy's fearful countenance and my right
eye could spy on my closest friend, whom I will call Steve, across the room.

The cover of Steve's paperback didn't seem to fit the rest of the book. Steve had been known to be destructive of books, while I tended to treat them like holy grails. He made me livid one day when he took the sharp point of a compass in geometry class and punched holes where David Copperfield's eyes were supposed to be. This time, however, the *Silas Marner* cover was intact. It just didn't fit. After glancing at Miss Purdy, I looked again and noted that the *Silas Marner* cover not only overlapped the edges of the pages but also didn't fit flush against the spine either. In fact, the spine itself had another cover snug against it. Then I understood: Steve was using the cover of *Silas Marner* as camouflage for another book!

Another of my friends—a boy across the street—hid his *Playboy*s in a closet trunk.

Miss Purdy was an excellent teacher. As a ninth grader, however, I didn't spend time praising her teaching; we speculated at length about her personal life. She was tall and statuesque and unmarried. She wore eyeglasses over a distinctive proboscis (my friend Doug had learned that word from his father after he first met Miss Purdy). She was also the daughter of a dentist about half the students in our class went to, and the knowledge that her father had put his hand down our throats made her very strange indeed. We also knew that she was no fool.

She began what looked like a leisurely stroll around the *U*-shaped arrangement of desks, only to pounce on Steve's book like a hawk.

"And what have we here?"

When he made a lame effort to recover the book, her stare turned him to stone. The bell rang, but we knew not to move. We watched, our collective breaths held, as she disdainfully set the *Silas Marner* cover on Steve's desk. She twisted Steve's ear until he stood up (in 1965 this was not an uncommon disciplinary habit), and she walked him toward her desk. I was of course concerned about my closest friend and the awful punishment that might await him, but I was more interested in the title of the book. It was called *Candy*. I was quick to gain a pirated copy and read it cover to cover as far away from Miss Purdy and my parents as possible. And I ever so briefly wondered—I immediately dismissed the thought from my mind—whether Miss Purdy had heard of the book. And if she knew anything about what went on in the book's pages.

Surely not. She was a teacher.

With Steve in tow, and turned at a dramatic angle so that the entire class could witness, Miss Purdy held *Candy* at arm's length and let it drop into the trash can beside her desk. Steve was then summarily ordered to the headmaster's office.

I am now that headmaster.

Lately, I have been thinking a lot about this grossly dated episode. Two months ago, some boys in the Lower School in class shared pornographic material with classmates and were discovered. The details of the episode are not important, but there's no mistaking the nature and the intent. Responding was difficult for all involved—students, teachers, and parents—and much more complicated than my best friend's clandestine attempt to read a banned book.

In 1965 *Playboy* or magazines similar to it were not sold to minors. Librarians would not check out certain books. My mother stayed home the entire time I was in school, and on occasion friends of my parents felt a strong enough obligation, in my parents' absence, to gently reprimand me about behavior of which they knew my parents disapproved. The personal computer and the Internet and cell phones didn't exist. When my parents allowed me to watch television, four channels were available. There were two telephones in the house, one of which my parents could pick up and tell me to hang up if I'd been talking too long with a girl. My hometown had a curfew. The time was in no ways perfect. I found ways to read *Candy*, I found ways to get in trouble, I found ways to disobey, all of which I should have done as part of growing up, but in 1965 the safety net, at least for a boy from a family like mine, was strung fairly tight. This is not news to anyone today.

Nor is it news that today's net is not tightly woven. Technology has knifed open the lives of boys. So have food, diet, and chemicals. Children are reaching puberty at a younger age than they did fifty years ago, when I did, and for those of us who are parents or grandparents, we know all too viscerally what epoch-making societal and cultural changes have occurred in this country between 1960 and now, some of which have been keenly important for social justice, others of which have challenged the very idea of community.

But instead of making grand pronouncements about a half century of cultural changes, or writing about something I don't know enough about, let me simply remind you of the mild and safe fact that began this letter: The book of choice for my English teachers was *Silas Marner*. It became *Catcher in the Rye* (OK, I love *Catcher*—well, sort of). In other words, we once read about a miser who turns good but replaced that story with the alienated teenager. We went from a protagonist who turns outward (Silas) to the protagonist who can't get out of himself (Holden). It's a small example but true.

I very much understand that growing up today is different from growing up when I was young—and radically different from the time when my parents were young. The Internet, in all its glory and its filth, is with us. Mindless films that celebrate violence are with us. At most recent count, there are twenty-five legal ways to watch television. Marketing built around sexual titillation is with us. On their magical phones, children will send naked pictures of themselves. They will slam and "slut" each other. Something else grossly vulgar and inappropriate lurks in Silicon Valley, month by month, soon to be accepted as everyday. It doesn't do any good for us as parents or teachers to be oblivious to the facts, for our children certainly aren't.

I can say little to parents but teach what's right. We will do the same. Let us work hard at it. School yourself, and keep the faith.

Parade Out the Gargoyles

What are these fantastic monsters doing in the cloisters under
the very eyes of the brothers as they read? What is the meaning
of these unclean monkeys, strange savage lions and monsters?
To what purpose are here placed these creatures, half beast,
half man? . . . Surely if we do not blush for such absurdities we
should at least regret what we have spent on them.

—St. Bernard of Clairvaux

*A*s a young man I once traveled for a fascinating but tough eleven weeks
through the Soviet Union, going east as far as Samarkand. I didn't shave
or get a haircut. When I broke free from the Iron Curtain, I boarded an
overnight train from Vienna to Paris and met two former roommates from
Ireland, who were so entertained by my grotesque looks they kept me from
cleaning up for another day. They took a photograph of me that my children
find particularly entertaining. In it, I have mounted the 387 steps up the
south tower of the Cathedral of Notre Dame and foolishly leaned over the
parapet of the Galerie des Chimères, my head positioned between two corner
gargoyles, both a fantastical blend of monkey, dog, pelican, and griffin. For
some reason, this was where I wanted my photo pasted into the archives of
my life. The question, of course, is who was uglier—the gargoyles, or the
scraggly young man two decades from becoming a headmaster, who most
days, some say, is fairly well scrubbed.

Gargoyles are a subset of the architectural carvings known as grotesques.
While gargoyles may be ugly, they nonetheless function as waterspouts de-
flecting rain from stonewalls (they "gargle"). But grotesques care less about
utility. They might deflect water off the tops of their heads but accidentally—
they don't intend to help. The stonemasons sculpted them, apparently, only

to ornament. But they and their cost distressed the most famous of abbots, Bernard of Clairvaux.

Some are beautiful. At our sister institution, Washington National Cathedral, 321 angels reside mainly on the central Gloria in Excelsis Tower. They do what we expect—sing praises to God and play instruments (but only the kind held close to the body so as to avoid the water damage their minions the gargoyles prevent elsewhere). One angel plays the upright piano in honor of Bishop John Walker. Another wears a baseball cap. One holds an Oscar statuette, and the best of all, in my theological opinion, fingers a die carved with the number seven.

But those most intriguing to tourists, like Darth Vader, Toothsome, and the Crooked Politician, are fearsome and ugly. They are indeed "grotesque."' Legend explains. In the seventh century, a priest named Romanus led the dragon La Gargouille to Rouen, slew the creature, and saved the city from its curse. The builders of the cathedral carved the face of the dragon on a waterspout of the building—hence, the first gargoyle.

But the answers to St. Bernard's question don't end with legend. The gargoyles probably boosted attendance (somewhat like a circus sideshow similar to an essential tourist trade). They might have lured pagans, demonstrated the conversion of evil to good, punished the wicked in their hearts, frightened evil spirits, and contrasted the dangerous outside with the safety and order inside the church. Those first designers and stone carvers, converted from paganism to Christianity, might have been hedging their bets (throw them bones!).

My youthful attraction to the gargoyles of Notre Dame makes perfect sense to me now. Let me stretch the metaphor, just for fun. Many people say that the most useful function of a school is to create a safe environment and nurture a child or build up his self-esteem. But disequilibrium is also necessary for learning. We assess what the child knows; move the child away from a preconceived idea; make him realize that ideas need to be broken apart and be made anew; and repeat the process. The gargoyles I look up at as I walk to work can spook us away from preconceived ideas (that a cathedral, for example, would be ornamented only with angels). They should dislodge us from our preconceptions and tip our intellectual and spiritual balance, but only as a way, in the end, for us to go inside to the nave to steady ourselves anew, to secure ourselves more firmly.

If I could teach a class every day—say, on a literary text we loved—where my students and I carefully constructed a cathedral of learning, laying our cruciform over the author's words from east to west, sculpting delicate Gothic arches from the text's images, coloring the space between the words with stained glass and filling them with the music of Bach, and then, when all the students, full of self-satisfaction, thought their task was over and our criticism of the text was perfect, I could successfully parade out the gargoyles and shock them—s*hock and unbalance* them—I would after one such class retire as an educator. By themselves my students would then pick up the pieces of their cathedral and rebuild it—it would stand on a firmer foundation—and I would lay claim in front of St. Peter to at least a corner niche in the Heavenly Academy of Learned Teachers.

But a gargoyle will be waiting there, to pinch me.

Scaffolding and Learning

We are constructing a new academic building. It goes well.

I borrow from the language of construction. For about one hundred years, the worlds of child development and education have made "scaffolding" an educational metaphor. A child must learn to solve problems, a goal central to teaching but also, I would argue, central to parenting, as long as we remind ourselves that the problems a child learns to solve in his family setting are less the skill of writing a coherent paragraph and more the skill of living a coherent life. To become a good problem-solver in both arenas, a child needs the temporary support of scaffolding.

We know as teachers and parents that there is a gap between the problems a child can solve alone and those he can solve in collaboration with adults. My emphasis is on "collaboration." A child can do a problem alone. An adult can do a problem alone. There is no collaboration if the adult does the problem for the child. The nature of a problem a child can solve alone as well as a problem a child can solve in collaboration with an adult changes according to the child's development. To be extreme, a six-year-old cannot yet write an essay appropriate for our Upper School's Expository Writing class.

Faced with these truths, as a teacher I try to keep the metaphor of scaffolding ever-present in my mind. For my students, this is the house I aspire for: First floor, I want them to love to learn; second floor, to love literature deeply; and third floor, to know how to read it and write about it with critical insight. I fail to collaborate on their house-building if on the first floor, instead of inspiring a child to love to learn, I tell him how much I know; on the second floor, instead of testing out what kind of literature inspires him, I rhapsodize solely about the literature that has moved me; and on the third, instead of creating situations where he must read and think about the answers

130

to my persistent use of the word "why," I answer all the questions myself, and instead of forcing him to figure out how to rewrite, I correct his errors myself.

I succeed as a teacher if I remind myself each day that I am not a great Ducal Palace on the Grand Canal charging admissions to gaze at my Titians. I am both a construction worker and an artist, and I hammer and nail the scaffolding for a child to help him build his own palace, knowing perfectly well that I have to work with him in stages, also knowing perfectly well that his palace does not have to be an exact copy of my palace or his neighbor's palace or, God forbid, an older sibling's. I provide a lot of scaffolding at the beginning. I provide less so as the child develops, until one day, after slowly removing parts of it, I remove all of it. Then I stand back and admire. Mission accomplished.

Son, great job. Stay in touch in college. And when you succeed with your adult palace, send money.

The truest insight, though, comes after I see him walk down the cathedral aisle at high school graduation and know the collaboration helped me just as much as it helped him. Please hold that thought.

Our children come to us with their own set of blueprints, which, by and large, we delight in. On occasion we wish they were not cursed with the threats of this uncle's alcoholic gene or that aunt's misanthropy or the most problematic genes that always seem to come down from your spouse's insane family. Making those blueprints real and truly human, however, is the most difficult task God gives us, as difficult, at the very least, as managing a multi-million-dollar corporation, performing brain surgery, or arguing in front of the Supreme Court. How do we raise a child so that he feels deeply loved and protected from the harsh winds of the world, but when he becomes an adult he wants to stand on his own foundation, as he should, and is capable of doing so? For remember, the ultimate goal of parenting is to make ourselves honored and loved and remembered, but ultimately unnecessary.

Let me return, if you will, to the thought I asked you to hold. A child comes into the world. Suddenly, not simply in our mind, but in our flesh and blood, we change. Women have felt themselves change over the course of nine months. For men the change is abrupt. Sons and daughters, miraculously we hold a baby in our arms and realize, *mirabile dictu*, that we have become fathers and mothers. Before / after: not reversible. God and nature charge us with this baby's literal survival, and our first response is to pour everything we have into him or her, providing the ground floor of a child's development. But then something happens. Slowly that child teaches us, and we begin to understand—that love begins to require that we learn restraint, requires us to learn to take some of ourselves away, like the slow removal of scaffolding.

Let me continue with this vein. If we believe our children need to be healthy, then we learn that as parents we must be more careful about the way we lead our own lives. We must lead healthy and safe lives in front of them and slowly and carefully let their world widen, in doing so inoculating them to disease. For them to be safe, we need to teach them how to handle dangerous situations when we are not there; to be happy, we feed our own happiness and share it with them, but we must also allow them to be sad and to be alone in their sadness, no matter how much it pains us to watch them suffer; for them to gain self-respect, we don't abuse ourselves in front of them, and we stop ourselves from praising them falsely; to be successful, we explain how failures led to our successes and let them fail on their own. Then we provide support for efforts to rise again. Finally, for them to love and be loved, we love each other in front of them and have the courage to let them suffer in their own loves. Soon enough, God willing, they will find the right love.

At the movies recently, I have noticed a fashion of short outtakes that roll during the final credits. I've picked up my jacket, tried to connect some of the actors with past films, looked for who wrote the music, and started to exit the theater only to have another little drama unfold that makes everyone stop in the aisles and turn back to the screen. I have used the metaphor of scaffolding only to remind us of the great challenge of teaching and parenting. As I conclude, imagine if you will, a short outtake. In the film all of us—boys, parents, faculty—stand or move about a building. Perhaps all of us are wearing hard hats, or even black hats and bonnets in honor of those religious communities that would gather together to raise a barn for the community, and we are smiling, laughing with each other, admiring the work, and because so many of us at this boys' school are men, we're probably indulging in a little horseplay, too. All of us together are responsible for raising a group of boys. They are boys we love now, boys who with our wise love—a love both of joy and of restraint—will become men and indeed builders themselves.

Look once more at that outtake before you go, at your son and at yourselves. How glorious to see that host of people, present and past, smiling on such handiwork.

• 37 •

The Freedom to Choose One's Way

We who lived in concentration camps can remember the men who walked through the huts comforting others, giving away their last piece of bread. They may have been few in number, but they offer sufficient proof that everything can be taken from a man but one thing: the last of the human freedoms—to choose one's attitude in any given set of circumstances, to choose one's own way.

—Victor Frankl

$\mathscr{L}$ate in August, as the school race begins, I contemplate the core mission of any school worth its salt. Let us gladly learn, as Chaucer's clerk said, and gladly teach. Our gladness makes a difference, does it not?

I write about a teacher named Johnson Mlambo. I do not write about Mr. Mlambo's gift of lecturing, though I have read enough of his work to know he has mastered rhetoric. I do not write about his gift of critical thinking and his ability to teach such thinking to his students, though I know he has an incisive intellect. Nor do I write of Mr. Mlambo's Socratic method or problem solving. Rather I write about Mr. Mlambo when he could not teach, at least formally.

The place where he served his prison time was near a limestone quarry, where prisoners spent hot days mining the stone and then by wheelbarrow returning it to the prison. Every time a guard named Piet was on duty, he stopped Mr. Mlambo, choked him until he was almost unconscious, dumped his wheelbarrow out, and made him return to the quarry to work extra hours, far more than any other prisoner was required to work. This was a routine punishment. What was not routine was what a group of guards did one day after work, because Mr. Mlambo had talked back to a guard and threatened him. They buried all of Mr. Mlambo except his head in the dirt next to the

133

quarry and then urinated on him. Another time in the prison mess, a guard hit Mr. Mlambo's arm while he was eating soup, the attack timed perfectly so that the soup spilled onto the prison warden's pants. The penalty for this was a whipping.

All the prisoners remember to this day the sound of the beating Mr. Mlambo received outside the prison yard. When he was led back into the yard, the man stood tall, showed no emotion on his face, returned to his position in line with the others, knelt by the stones he was instructed to break apart with a pickax, and did so without once letting on about the pain he was suffering from his bloodied back. Finally, I will not tell you the last story I discovered about Mr. Johnson Mlambo, only to say that the results of that torture and trip to the mainland hospital led to his now having a glass eye.

Why such mistreatment? Why mistreatment that the other prisoners write was much worse than what they suffered?

I stood in a group of seven people in the middle of a nondescript prison yard—forty by twenty meters, with dully painted concrete walls, barred windows on small cells, and no vegetation. Above all a wide African sky burned. We had come to Robben Island, one of the most famous prisons in the world, the island off the shore of Cape Town, South Africa, where Nelson Mandela was kept for thirty-one years prior to announcing upon his release that the way to make a new democracy in South Africa was not through revenge and retribution but through truth and reconciliation.

Hollywood gets evil wrong when it paints and sings only of the glorious battlefields of *Lord of the Rings*. Evil lies in dirty and depressing yards, in nondescript rooms, in the common and the everyday.

Standing in that yard, I listened to a passionate speech by Eddie Daniels, a prisoner whose everyday dog-like cell was across from Walter Sisulu, a few separate from our teacher Johnson Mlambo, and one or two more away from a solicitor named Nelson Mandela. Eddie Daniels knew we were school people. He had been put in prison when he was eighteen but came out twenty-five years later with a college education by correspondence. Here was a man who truly valued education. Of course he wanted to answer our questions about Nelson Mandela, but he wanted to tell us in particular about his friend Johnson Mlambo.

He explained that when Johnson arrived at the island by boat, he knelt down in front of the guards with twenty-five or so other prisoners. The warden of the prison stood behind each of the kneeling prisoners, identity papers in hand, as the guards stood in front of them looking on. The warden then went down the line, one by one, explaining to the guards the background of each—rapist, murderer, thief, and in some cases like Johnson Mlambo's, political prisoner. It was part of the strategy of the apartheid government to imprison political prisoners with criminals. When the warden stood behind

Johnson Mlambo, he said, "And this is our most dangerous prisoner." The warden paused. "Why? Because he's a teacher."

I have carried that story with me back home. Why would a group of prison guards and their warden believe that a teacher could be their most dangerous prisoner? Wouldn't it be a rapist, a murderer, or a gangster? Why a teacher?

When I engaged Mr. Eddie Daniels about that question on the ferry trip back to Cape Town, he said this to me: "Yes, they treated him worse than any other prisoner. He knew ideas. Nothing scared them more than black intellectuals. And if a person is a black intellectual and he is really good at spreading ideas around to other people and convincing them they should study political theory, learn maths and science, and read the classics, then he is a very dangerous person indeed. What would that do to a political system based on the color of your skin?"

All of us teaching at St. Albans are privileged. While some of us have suffered at the hands of racism, usually but not always in subtle ways, none of us have suffered prison, even as a result of racism or our political beliefs. As severe as segregation has been on our African American teachers my age, apartheid's injustices were even more brutal than an Alabama sheriff named Bull O'Connor's and much more systematic than our government's. Imagine, a life of breaking stones.

Teaching is powerful and can even be a dangerous vocation. It calls us to lead young people out of themselves and out of their false securities. We hope to lead them into a disposition toward life they are not naturally inclined to, one not of taking and bullying and being selfish, but of seeking justice and compassion for all, of giving and sacrificing and caring.

The Viennese psychotherapist Victor Frankl, released from a Nazi concentration camp at the end of the war, argued that everything can be taken from a person, but the most essential of human freedoms, in any set of circumstances, privileged or deprived, is the freedom to choose one's own attitude. The truth, the Gospel says, will set us free.

I realize the dangers of using such analogy in the middle of such privilege as ours: a prison in South Africa, a concentration camp, a school high on a hill overlooking the capital of the United States. But each September, we meet again a new generation of boys and, in our case, many are the sons of the very powerful in this very powerful nation. They can be taught the right skills but they must also be moved to right action. They must first see our example—that we believe the boy in the next desk not from a wealthy family is just as important as the wealthy boy next to him. Then they can be moved by our words about the lessons of history or the parables of scripture. Teaching is, in any circumstance, a powerful and sacred venture. We have it easy, yes, but let that benefit challenge us all the more.

· 38 ·

Let the Children Come

*I*n the gospel reading, the Master calls, "Let the children come unto me." He says we see in them the kingdom of God.

We know teaching takes place everywhere—not simply in the classroom but in studio, athletic field, office, hallway (most especially), downtown, outer space, and home. If done right, teaching exhausts. It frustrates and is supremely glorious. It's never the same from one day to the next. Boredom is not allowed.

Good teaching strives to be at least a "soft" science, in the sense that we try to find a method to our madness. We are taught to ask: What enables learning? We formulate hypotheses about the effectiveness of a lesson, and we test the results, modify our formulation, and start again. If today's lesson causes completely unexpected misunderstanding ("You think I said that?") or those "Oh-gag-I'm-bored-to-tears" looks, tomorrow we try another method. It might inspire the sorely desired "Aha!" moment in a child's eyes.

Teaching is also an art. In his essay "The Crack-up" (1936), F. Scott Fitzgerald famously said, "The test of a first-rate intelligence is the ability to hold two opposed ideas in the mind at the same time, and still retain the ability to function." A teacher's challenge is analogous, except that you hold about twenty fidgety or hormone-bursting youths and their opposed ideas, or absence thereof, in mind during the same lesson. You function. Message to self: must do more than function. In the middle of that buzzing class or practice session, you try to make connections that work for each child.

Teaching is also a great human enterprise. We always and sometimes smugly cite Henry Adams and his "teaching affects eternity," but he was on to something—our work can last through at least a generation. Every adult carries around inside his head a memory about some teacher who inspired him.

Before that adult dies, he will pass that story on. Sometimes those stories detail intellectual growth ("She taught me to be a historian" or "He taught me how to argue a point") but most often those stories we remember speak of emotional attention. She cared for me after we lost, he talked to me when I was lonely, he carried me atop his back, he loved me when I felt empty, she disciplined me when that was what I most needed, she challenged me to believe in my ability, and he said something I've never forgotten.

And all of us walk around the product of teachers' work that we might not acknowledge and certainly don't sentimentalize. Nevertheless, the positive work might show itself in how we solve problems, organize ourselves, remember rules, or recall information.

It is this seed of eternity that *all* teachers are called to hold in a trust, timeless and sacred. We must weigh, then, what is best now but also long-lasting for our students, and we must be reminded of the students who have gone before—the people of our generation and our fathers' and mothers' generation—and we must strengthen the school for the students yet to come.

So each fall, they come here as they have come in the past and will come in the future, full of varsity desire and new ideas, clothed in pretense and cool and—thank God—even in innocence. Deep beyond their disguises into their hearts, they're searching. Perhaps that's what the kingdom of God is?

· 39 ·

The Eagle and the Selfies

In another blessed moment in this privileged life I've been given, I stood with my thirty-year-old son Evan at the rood screen and stared in awe at the Exeter College chapel at Oxford. A step from us perched an ornate lectern with its sculpture of Isaiah's golden eagle cradling the scripture. Ahead of us lay the wooden stalls of the choir, with the insignias of Oxford colleges in each of the back row's niches, and the torch-lit altar awaited us at the far end, nestled in a semicircular east wall boasting glorious stained glass of the high Victorian era. The colors were rich, the wood warm, and the effect mesmerizing: sacred space indeed.

We're standing there, both in awe and in silence, for we need time to take it in, to let its majesty resonate. But as we studied it, we heard the grand doors behind and to the side of us open and the air change. The Book of Revelation speaks of the whirlwind. Three long-legged, chat-happy teenage girls burst in, one still wearing braces, all in shorts and fashionable rags, all with cell phones at work in their hands. We didn't have time to move out of the way. They blew by and around us to stand not more than three steps ahead, beside the lectern and its eagle. They looked the place over.

Done.

Then they turned toward the open Scripture atop the shiny golden eagle. Two perched on one side of the eagle's face, one to the other side, and all three held up their cell phones to position the shot. All three kissed the cheeks of the eagle. Then snap, snap, snap. Three simultaneous selfies, kissing the old bird, and then they ran out, giggling.

I turned to Evan. "I think I have a homily," I said.

I have only two observations to make. Each originates out of reactions I felt myself experience in this visitation conducted by the angels, disguised

138

as three teenage girls. The first comes from my dark side, the usually cranky, too old, and over-intellectualized self who starts to cite Oswald Spengler's *The Decline of the West* and sees in these chatty girls the decline of decorum, the fall of the Christian church, the end of literacy, the loss of civilization itself, and the doom of humankind. If you need any elaboration of this point of view, I have some friends on the faculty who can fill in the details.

In contrast to my dark side's response, I wouldn't necessarily say this comes from my sunny side, for all of you know me too well for me to try to convince you I have one. But perhaps it comes from the best part of my teacher's self. Isn't this a good story for us teachers to use as a warm-up exercise for the year ahead?

And so each fall, we are blessed once more with the charge to civilize, against all odds. We teach good manners, good character, and good thought. We teach that the self is less found in a selfie than in the face of the Other. And we are charged to be patient, endlessly patient.

My son later said that he imagined the three girls were on a scavenger hunt scripted by a fellow teacher, a common practice in the summers in Oxford, a possibility that somehow makes my patience with them kick in. *Of course*, I think—actually following instructions.

But we don't need to know. Nor do fellow teachers need me preaching about patience: You're experienced in this business, and many of you are parents, where patience is the only way to survive.

My Students, Now

*M*y reading list intimidates, but my students are whip-smart. I marvel at so much about them: their faith that the world can be changed, their obsessive multitasking, the speed with which they navigate each new technology that lives only to die and reappear again, the range of cultures they're familiar with, often learned because of their breadth of knowledge about popular culture, now a worldwide construct. I might have had a favorite Beatle and that's it.

They argue, are witty, often listen, and learn even as they are too cool to admit it. The boys love fast video games, many intensely violent; the boys and girls like teachers who use constant video and slides and create websites and tweet at-home office hours; most prefer film (watched on computers or phones) to books, and they're schooled in scene changes and short plot points—beats, as the screenwriters say—especially as compared to leisurely PBS scenes, a channel they know only from *Sesame Street* (ironically moved now to HBO). Forget a nineteenth-century novel, where I still find a home. They can easily read long novels—consider the *Harry Potter* series and all the vampires and *The Hunger Games*—but in each case plot trumps present-day social concerns and character development, which resides comfortably and all too unfortunately in stereotype.

They don't grumble about advertisements the way I do. They laugh at my diatribes against incessant marketing. They accept entertainment as news and are fascinated when I cite some critic who dates the beginning of the downfall of the news industry to Marilyn Monroe's doing the birthday sultry to John Kennedy. They very much prefer prose with words that click, a funhouse of mirrors in which I lose my mind. The world is multiple, and multiplying, not singular, whether in multitasking or belief. When asked to explain an allusion to the Judeo-Christian tradition or classical literature, they stumble (unless it's revealed in a video game), feel a little guilty (which I make worse), and then, behind my back, smile at my outdated outrage and total cluelessness about contemporary culture: in particular, about music and celebrities. They are comfortable reading about two-thirds the length of an exact assignment I made thirty to forty years ago (to their parents). And yet they're smart, eager, and inquisitive.

Sometimes I slip into the same school of thought I hated in the generation ahead of me: "the decline school." If I remember assigning the opening of *Paradise Lost* in 1974 and imagine assigning and teaching the same passage now, I forgive myself for joining the apostles of despair. I'd be crazy to try again (which doesn't mean I won't). I must guard against this despair. Memory is unreliable. Did they actually read and understand Milton or was I just clueless about teaching having something to do with their learning and not my erudition as I pattered on explaining the incredible number of Hebraic and Hellenic allusions in only two or three lines, all the while so self-satisfied. I cringe at the memory of so much, but especially what I must have sounded like. But still, I do give credence to recent journalism that posits our brains and our skill sets are changing more rapidly than we imagine. We are reading in different ways. I watch and see, and today I do a much better job of studying the evidence in others. But I hesitate to say that change is necessarily for the worse. That's for future thinkers to study the indications they'll have. I do know these "kids" are smart and I remain optimistic about their intellectual futures.

I write this as another school year begins. In my opinion, I'm fortunate to be at an established school. Reading the previous paragraphs, you can see I only read the negative connotations of the metaphor "cutting edge." Our school is "old," but by Mid-Atlantic and not New England standards, and one that cherishes traditions, perhaps too self-referentially and even self-reverently. While we don't reinvent ourselves each September, we should remind ourselves that our students do. In these nine years under our tutelage, every aspect of their bodies, minds, and souls endures and, we hope, thrives with the greatest changes of their entire lives.

And so each September we must realize that we do need to begin anew. Year one, followed by year one.

There is a universal school quip using the concept of water. You know it. It usually refers to the makeup of a group, most often an entire class. Sometimes it's negative (My goodness, what was in the water *that* year?) and other times positive (Boy, what *was* in the water that year?). A few days ago, in fact, a parent at a dinner party explained to me that the disruption in one son's class paralleled the disruptions in the same classes in schools throughout the area—a bad birth lot, in other words. That universality was only matched by the delight she and her friends felt in their younger sons' classes—some good kids, she explained. Then she referenced Chinese mystical symbolism on the year a person is born.

I'm a Leo, but who's to say?

I will say this, that it remains a great challenge to teach, especially because the water does vary year after year. I clarify: It is a great challenge as long as you are doing it the right way. You have to begin with your students' emotions and know that as much as your emotions might be caught up in a lifetime study of your subject, they are human beings who do not yet know the kind of disciplined love for the work you have. So you begin with the need to inspire with stories about the material that somehow relates to their experience and patience as you move toward the business at hand. There are great stories to tell about every intellectual pursuit. In other words, you can't let your willingness to listen and accept the place "where they're coming from" turn into another rap session about relevance in their lives.

Thus, to the work. Your students are going to construct their own learning, and each night you kneel and pray that each one's build of the course content that day and tomorrow has some semblance to your understanding. To use an athletic metaphor, you hope that their understanding is at least in the same ballpark as yours. And as a teacher, you also provide assessments beyond the ones you create so that your teaching and their learning may be evaluated by professionals whose expertise creates standards in the field. These "outside" assessments—standardized tests being the most common—do not replace or trump your assessment as the day-to-day professional. But I am of the school that teachers who don't use "outside" assessments have too much confidence in their own abilities.

So to inspire your students to construct their learning well enough not to collapse in a rubble of delusion, you use every pedagogical tool available to you, from lecture to discussion, small group to whole, from visuals and talking websites and talking heads to using the hands and the heart—anything that might help a student feel and know the beat of the course, the excitement of the material, the way to put together an essay or defense, solve a problem, translate a passage, or sing and hop on one leg. And you anchor your efforts in limitless listening and questioning in return, and you encourage in them and in you a truthful assessment of work, original and revised, even assessing all efforts in and out of class, including simply talk. You are tasked with inspiring learning and in the process determining what the student knows and how best to keep that student's dance dancing.

This glorious vocation demands all of you: daily thoughtfulness and study, careful preparation and insightful on-the-fly assessment, patience beyond measure, resilience against exhaustion and despair, and, most essentially, the disposition when the work is real and good to be joyful, each in his or her own teacher-ly way.

What We Desire

$\mathcal{I}$ was having lunch last year in New York with a thirty-two-year-old St. Albans graduate whom I taught his senior year. We sat across from each other in a stunning rooftop setting: glass office-building walls glimmering from sunlight above the Hudson, taxi-horn blasts echoing up from canyons below, a tern gliding in the wind tunnel between the monumental glories of the great city. For the first fifteen minutes of lunch, when he chowed down in a way I too viscerally remembered and envied, all was routine. We noted the view, caught up on school (oh the aggrieved jealousy of young alums when they see the new athletic fields), passed the classmate gossip, and considered the campaign.

Yes, even at thirty-two, he and the financial industry had already danced together. "You can spread a gift out over five years," I said.

But he looked worried. "I had a dream."

I resisted the line. It didn't feel like an avoidance tactic.

"Just last night."

"You knew I would ask about the campaign?"

He didn't smile.

Well, that didn't work.

"I was caught in a crowd of a hundred, maybe. In the middle was a speaker. He was like a rabbi or teacher or someone with wisdom. No, Wisdom with a capital *W*. Everyone was straining to hear and I was scared about what he was saying even though I didn't hear the exact words. I didn't know why. What do they call it, free-floating . . ."

"Anxiety." Vainly, I kept trying to lighten the mood. "Never known it myself."

But once again, this young man needed to be serious, even in the glories of this incredible day high up among the mirrors of the American workplace. And it became my business, as it is for all of us, to pay attention.

"There was a terror in my soul."

One of the battalions of terrors in my soul when I accepted the job as St. Albans' headmaster was that three of my predecessors, from 1949 until 1997, were priests, trained in counseling and far more comfortable than I was in the call of a supplicant's anxiety and response from the faith of the headmaster. I could read literature and go left on the basketball court and try not to be accused of false modesty.

I repeated the words. "A terror in your soul?"

He shifted a fork from one side of his plate to the other and laid his open hand flat on his chest, heart level. "An animal pouncing in the night."

I sipped water.

"I woke up because it jumped on my chest."

"Yes."

"And it happened while I was in the crowd. People looked at me but weren't scared of the animal. They scorned me as if I had made some kind of embarrassing faux pas. Can't you listen? they asked."

He picked his napkin off his lap and carefully folded it. "Mr. Wilson, I am very successful. Our school prepared me well."

Now I knew how to answer. "Our lasting strength has been generations of great teachers. You should thank them."

"I'm thirty-two and have more money than I know what to do with," he said.

"Has that become a bad thing?" I queried.

By the standards of a life-long teacher, I thought, I began to make what felt like very good money when I turned forty-nine. It has been deeply, deeply appreciated. It changed my life, mostly, I pray, in positive ways, but without a doubt it changed me. We deceive ourselves if we think it does not.

"I am fiercely depressed."

I paused. All of us pause before we respond. "You've sought help?"

He didn't answer me but said, "I guess I want *everything*, Mr. Wilson."

Reduced to repetition again. "*Everything?*"

"In the world I live in, some of my bosses can own nearly anything they can dream of. You've seen the ship Tiger Woods owns? One of our guys owns the equivalent but just isn't public about it. Another owns an island. I'm serious. They've made it into a bird sanctuary. One guy has houses on the Upper East Side, Montauk, London, and the Loire Valley, and a staff at each who prepare every day of the week for their unannounced arrival, in case he and whoever have a whim to fly away on his helicopter or jet."

I knew what I was supposed to say, what my position called for me to say. I grew up schooled in Christ's words about the rich man and the needle to heaven and had sat through one waffling sermon after another about it. I knew at least the same number of his examples of very wealthy people, most of whom I've met in independent school trustee and parent circles, who are as deeply unhappy as this young man but yet they were my age—and in a despair they try to ease with each new mansion, each new affair, and each new trip. But I didn't want to be false in any way, about what I would do with an island of my own or how I'd sacrilegiously compare a flat in London to heaven. I didn't want to fall back into an acceptable answer for a head of a church school to speak if I didn't embrace my own words. If I just didn't know the addictive nature of money, I might be able to do that without guilt. In fact, who doesn't want *everything*?

Well . . . OK . . . I admit. Some people don't. A few.

"That must be quite a life some of them lead," I said. "Might appear perfect."

"Some are clearly unhappy, though," he said.

Perhaps he would provide what should be said.

"But others are really pleasant people—nice guys, deeply helpful—and in many ways use their money for good, like giving to their schools."

I smiled. "Am I supposed to say touché?"

"No, not at all. I am going to give. I owe so much."

"Thank you."

"You know, even with this wealth I describe, they still work very hard."

"I'm not surprised. To use your example, I suspect few people have trained as hard as Tiger Woods."

He touched his shoulders. "But this is about me."

I laughed, and he wasn't offended. "It's always about us, isn't it?"

But then the veil fell again—it shot down as if he were embarrassed to laugh—a dark mask inset his eyes. I was shocked at the change. I wasn't certain anything I said for the next few minutes would penetrate what just happened. He had claimed that a very bad dream revealed his daily depression to him like a divine visitation (actually, was this his claim? I couldn't be sure). For a while the tone of the conversation, with its descriptions of the places we can go, so to speak, and the nature of those in charge, made me think he was not in the ditch of despair he claimed. Yet the mask of his face began to worry me.

And then I was surprised again.

I thought forty years in my profession had schooled me to predict when the so-called answer to life, from across the table, is going to come out of another person's mouth. Let me explain. I have been reading job inquiries since I was a division head at the age of twenty-seven. Twenty years before coming to St. Albans, in fact, I ran a division of a placement company in the South and spent my days talking to people about teaching in independent schools. I tend to pick on lawyers when I tell this story, for they are the most frequent nontraditional applicants, but I have read inquiry letters from nearly every vocation that requires a B.A. Some of our greatest faculty members are former lawyers, scientists, businesspeople, med students, professional athletes, farmers, and more. But a certain, all-too-prevalent tone in the inquiry letters makes me feel when I read them like my office suffers an infestation of chiggers. And suddenly the same tone came from this young man I deeply admired when I taught him, and in this very moment I was both impressed by him and worried. But I also felt, and so many of us as teachers suffer the same emotion, that he hadn't paid attention to a word I said.

"I'm thinking, Mr. Wilson, about shucking it all and becoming a teacher."

My guards popped up like the armor of a transformer toy.

I needed to be careful, no question. I do believe in the ministerial aspect of my work—my calling, even if I am not a priest, to listen with an open mind, not one warped by experience and prejudice. But his words beat on my heart, too.

All one shucks to become a teacher, I kept myself from saying, is a good salary for one equivalent to that of a Washington, D.C., Metro bus driver. What remains is the simple fact of life that you get up in the mornings and still look in the mirror when you shave or do your face. You still suffer the injustices of people who short sell. Some days you short sell the lives of children and go home in despair. And then you dream yourself that there's another answer to this life we lead, the perfect answer, because when you think about it, you know that guy you went to school with, who couldn't write a paper without your help, now works in Lower Manhattan and looks from his office at the distant sails in the Sound as the Bloomberg indexes show that day after day his clients and he have enough money for the next trek to Patagonia and box seats at Yankee Stadium or the Met.

"It's not a question about teaching, Son."

Occasionally I slip into the privileges of age: *Son.* Perhaps it's also a defense mechanism.

The mask broke. He was used to my listening to his answers and opinions about our texts and asking follow-up questions, not responding with a bold declarative sentence.

"How do you mean?"

"It's a question of love."

He didn't get lost. Maybe we knew a similar cord of thinking, of feeling.

"Love? Defined as?"

"How, when you spend your time, you lose yourself. If what you lose yourself in brings good to another person and into the world, with the disclaimer that you should pull no selfish punches when you decide what good is and you must remember no pursuit is as pure as its defenders claim, then go for it. Go all in."

We were the last table occupied, still sitting, talking, on our second cappuccino. More than once he admitted he was late getting back to the office. In New York, there was no time of day (or of night when I was young enough to partake in that life and survive my dreams and delusions) that I didn't see someone in a restaurant eating or drinking. But strangely, this one near the clouds was done. We were alone, mid-afternoon, with everyone around us returned to their glassy cells or the muscular streets, the two of us departing this terraced restaurant, a single waiter in a tux, with a moustache, in a shaded corner, sneaking a peak at his cell phone.

My young friend spoke. "I was going to write you. You know I majored in classics?"

I laughed. "And with that you've become a wizard of Wall Street?"

He smiled. Thank God, he smiled. "And what is the perfect life, Mr. Wilson?"

I tilted my head, as if to say "Who knows?" and motioned to the man in the corner for the check. "I think St. Albans will take care of this one."

Acknowledgments

To begin, I must thank Molly Meinhardt, director of communications at St. Albans and my personal editor, whose book this also is. Patient, diligent, and wise, Molly has edited my errors, sharpened my thinking, and guided my approach to this collection. She is also a fine human being whom all of us at St. Albans love to work with. I count her as a close friend.

Faculty emeritus Paul Piazza—long-time associate head of school, English department chair, *Washington Post* reviewer of mysteries, and author of a book on Christopher Isherwood—edited my letters when I first began at St. Albans and for many years thereafter. I have deeply admired Paul for all his teaching and leadership and thank him for his efforts on my behalf.

However much help Molly and Paul have given me, the final draft's inelegancies or mistakes are mine and mine alone.

Ann Owens and Pam Grant have been the best administrative assistants a school head could desire. Their efforts at sorting through, editing, and organizing the many demands of a school head's work made finding the time to write this book possible. Both have been deeply loved by the school community.

I will not name other names, for the obvious reasons of accidentally leaving someone out, but so many teachers at school and colleagues around the Close have encouraged me, and I have deeply profited by the examples of my fellow school heads around the country and the world, especially those involved in the International Boys' Schools Coalition.

I give my love to Erin Meyer Wilson, who cherishes my son and has become a close friend. Thank you to Linda Dager Hall for her love and support in this difficult job. My mother and father would be proud of the book, while Mom would have corrected my theological backsliding. Any moral standing came from them. And I give thanks for my wonderful older brother, who was always proud of me and who was a pilot and a preacher of great renown—how I miss you.

And I return to Emily and Evan, anchors to my living. All my love, from Dad.

Index

Abraham, 11, 44, 58
Adam and Eve, 17–18
advertising. *See* marketing
afterlife, 103
alcohol, 71–73
angels, 44, 52, 58, 110, 128, 138
Anna Karenina, 97–98
Asheville School, 85
Asheville, N.C., 42–44
Auden, W.H., 13

beliefs, religious, denial or loss of, 18,
    51, 59–61
Benedict of Nursia, 24
Benedictine rule, 24–25
Buechner, Frederick, 21
Blanco, Numa, 8–9
Bonhoeffer, Dietrich, 65–67
boys, education of, 10, 12, 14, 15, 30–
    33, 119–120, 125, 132, 135, 140–41
brotherhood, 14–15
Bryan, William Jennings, 17, 43, 69–70
Bryn Mawr School, 31
Budde, Mariann, 24, 88, 100
Butler, James, Earl of Ormond, 84

Cain and Abel, 12
Catcher in the Rye, 125
celebrity. *See* fame

Coles, Robert, 27
college, preparation for, 110
Commission on Children at Risk,
    118–19
community, 5, 119–20
compassion, 91
courage, 65–66, 84, 98
Csikszentmihalyi, Mihaly, 39–41

Daily Office, 79
Daniels, Eddie, 134–35
Davis, John, 109, 115
death, 9, 51, 57, 60, 71, 79, 100, 103
dehumanization, survival of, 3
depression, 45–47
Diaz, Judy, 8–9
disaster, 53–54
Dun, Angus, 77–78

Eder, Craig, 115
education, 31–32, 109, 123–26
education, classical, 35
education, over-specialization of, 35
Eliot, George, 27, 99, 123
Eliot, T. S., 23
Emerson, Ralph Waldo, 44
escape, 98
evil, 97–98
Exeter College Chapel, Oxford, 138–39

151

About the Author

Mr. Z. Vance Wilson has served as the seventh headmaster of St. Albans School since July 1999.

Born in North Carolina, on August 8, 1950, and raised in Tampa, Florida, he attended Berkeley Preparatory School and earned his B.A. in English from Yale University, where he played varsity basketball and was nominated for a Rhodes Scholarship. He went on to earn a diploma in Anglo-Irish literature from Trinity College, University of Dublin, and a master's degree from the University of Virginia.

He began his teaching career in 1974 at the Lovett School in Atlanta, where he was quickly promoted to head of the Upper School. Subsequently, he worked as a teacher and administrator at Asheville School in Asheville, North Carolina, Tower Hill School in Wilmington, Delaware, and Bryn Mawr School in Baltimore, where he was the associate head. He also taught English at Madison Area Technical College.

Mr. Wilson recently served as president of the International Boys' Schools Coalition (IBSC) and is a former member of the governing board of Roxbury Latin School. He also belongs to the Headmasters' Association and the Country Day Heads Association.

Mr. Wilson has pursued a second career as a writer. He has co-authored two books on curriculum issues (*Paths to New Curriculum* and *Taking Measure*) and an account of integration in Southern private schools. In 1986 he published a novel, *The Quick and the Dead*.